Printed in Canada by Hemlock Printers

Contact: contact@first15.org
www.first15.org

Designed by Matt Ravenelle
mattravenelle.com

ABOUT FIRST15

Spending time alone with God every day can be a struggle. We're busier – and more stressed – than ever. But still, we know it's important to spend time alone with our Creator. We know we need to read his word, pray, and worship him.

First15 bridges the gap between desire and reality, helping you establish the rhythm of meaningful, daily experiences in God's presence. First15 answers the critical questions:

• Why should I spend time alone with God?
• How do I spend time alone with God?
• How do I get the most out of my time alone with God?
• How can I become more consistent with my time alone with God?

And by answering these questions through the format of daily devotionals, you'll practice the rhythm of meeting with God while experiencing the incredible gift of his loving presence given to those who make time to meet with him.

Allow God's passionate pursuit to draw you in across the next several days. And watch as every day is better than the last as your life is built on the solid foundation of God's love through the power of consistent, meaningful time alone with him.

To learn more about First15, visit our website first15. org. First15 is available across mobile app, email, podcast, and our website. Subscribe to our devotional today and experience God in a fresh way every day.

———

ABOUT THE AUTHOR

Craig Denison is the author of First15, a daily devotional guiding over a million believers into a fresh experience with God every day. In 2015, Craig founded First15 after sensing a longing in God's heart for his people to be about relationship – real, restored relationship with him – that above all else, he simply wanted the hearts of his people. Craig began praying, dreaming, and writing. And the idea of helping people spend the first fifteen minutes of their day focusing on nothing else but growing in their relationship with God was born. The vision was birthed in Craig's heart that if we as a people would worship, read, and pray at the beginning of every day, everything could change for the better. Craig writes, speaks, and he and his wife, Rachel lead worship to help believers establish a more tangible, meaningful connection with God.

———————

CONTENTS

**Building Blocks for
Your Time with God**
Week 1

**Why Spend Time
Alone with God?**
Week 2

**Centering Your Life Around
Meeting with God**
Week 3

**God Longs to be
Encountered**
Week 4

**Abiding in the
True Vine**
Week 5

Day 1 - What Does It Mean to Have Time Alone with God?   12-15

Day 2 - What is Worship?   16-19

Day 3 - What is a Devotional?   20-23

Day 4 - What is Prayer?   24-27

Day 5 - Communion with God   28-31

Day 6 - The Presence of God   32-35

Day 7 - What is Christian Meditation?   36-39

Day 8 - Start Your Day with the Best Thing   46-49

Day 9 - Storing the Treasure of Your Heart in Heaven   50-53

Day 10 - Live for Love   54-57

Day 11 - Renewing Your Mind   58-61

Day 12 - Having Time Alone   62-65

Day 13 - Life in Surrender   66-69

Day 14 - Freedom through Enjoying God   70-73

Day 15 - Choosing a Center   80-83

Day 16 - The Longing of God to Meet with You   84-87

Day 17 - Seeing God as Our Father   88-91

Day 18 - The Fruit of Abiding   92-95

Day 19 - Jesus is the Center   96-99

Day 20 - Making the Most of Our Time   100-103

Day 21 - Living from Union   104-107

Day 22 - Choosing a Center   114-117

Day 23 - The Longing of God to Meet with You   118-120

Day 24 - Seeing God as Our Father   122-125

Day 25 - The Fruit of Abiding   126-129

Day 26 - Jesus is the Center   130-133

Day 27 - Making the Most of Our Time   134-137

Day 28 - Living from Union   138-141

Day 29 - Choosing a Center   148-151

Day 30 - The Longing of God to Meet with You   152-155

Day 31 - Seeing God as Our Father   156-159

Day 32 - The Fruit of Abiding   160-163

Day 33 - Jesus is the Center   164-167

Day 34 - Making the Most of Our Time   168-171

Day 35 - Living from Union   172-175

Building blocks for your time with God

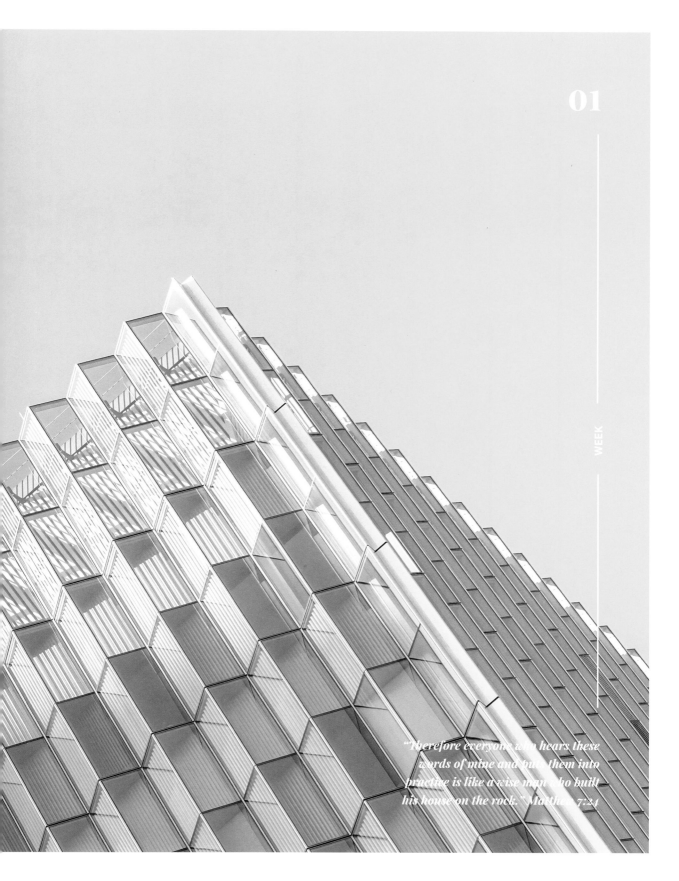

01

WEEK

"Therefore everyone who hears these words of mine and puts them into practice is like a wise man who built his house on the rock." Matthew 7:24

WEEKLY OVERVIEW

This week we'll spend time breaking down the individual components of First15 by sharing God's desire for each of them. The majority of First15 is dedicated to encountering God and learning about his character, but every now and then we will cover some teaching and tools that will help in pursuing God to greater depths. This week we will get back to the basics and learn some spiritual disciplines that will help us encounter him in deeper, more transformative ways.

What Does It Mean to Have Time Alone with God?

DEVOTIONAL

We all have a hunger to know why we're here. We all possess an insatiable desire for love, passion, and purpose. Maybe you've had a relationship with God for years. Maybe you're still trying to figure out if God even exists or if he is knowable. Wherever you are in your journey with God, know this—God longs to satisfy your hunger. He knows everything about you. He's counted every hair on your head and thinks about you more than the grains of sand (Psalm 139:18). And he loves you more than you could ever comprehend. So great is his steadfast love for you that he has a perfect plan for every one of your days. He longs to transform your thoughts, emotions. and actions with his loving kindness that your life may be filled with passion, purpose, satisfaction, and the wonderful peace of his presence.

"You have said, 'Seek my face.' My heart
says to you, 'Your face, Lord, do I seek."

PSALM 27:8

We all require transformation. We all need the freedom and healing that comes from relationship with our Creator. And we serve a God of miraculous transformation. Scripture says, *"God formed Man out of dirt from the ground and blew into his nostrils the breath of life. The Man came alive — a living soul!"* (Genesis 2:7 MSG). Psalm 139:13 states that God knit you together in your mother's womb. You are fearfully and wonderfully made for relationship with your heavenly Father (Psalm 139:14). Your heavenly Father longs to bring about miraculous transformation every day of your life so that you would be increasingly marked by the powerful work of his presence.

So how does God desire to bring about transformation? What are his perfect plans for filling your days with passion, purpose, and love? God's main avenue for transformation is through spending time alone with him every day. No matter where you are in your relationship with God, time spent in the presence of your Creator receiving a tangible revelation of his steadfast love will be the catalyst to living a life transformed. Just as a candle must be ignited with a flame to burn, so you must continuously encounter the fire of God's love to live a transformed, joy-filled life. He is the only constant source that you have. You will only find lasting satisfaction through his nearness. Nothing else will supply all you need to live the life you truly desire.

That's what First15 is all about. First15 was created to give you a practical resource to meet God every day. No matter how busy you are, you can set aside fifteen minutes to connect with your Creator and Sustainer. God longs to meet with you. He waits patiently to spend time with you. Think of that! The Creator of the universe, of all things wonderful and good, is patiently waiting right now to spend time with you!

The choice of how you will spend this year is entirely up to you. I pray that you would be filled with the longing and strength to spend time with your heavenly Father. I pray that this resource is helpful in connecting you to the Father that your longings would be fully satisfied in meeting with him. God is a limitless ocean of grace and help. And all that's necessary to receive from him is some time, open hands and an open heart. God calls you his beloved and longs for you to know to greater depths *"the breadth and length and height and depth"* of his great love for you (Ephesians 3:18).

Spend some time in guided prayer receiving the love of God. Answer the call to seek his face as David did in Psalm 27 saying, *"Your face Lord do I seek."*

GUIDED PRAYER

1. Take some time to ask God how he feels about you. God still speaks today. Jesus is still alive and at work through the Holy Spirit. The Spirit loves to speak to us. He loves to reveal God's heart. God is not silent. Simply make space to listen. Don't be frustrated if it's difficult at first. Listening to God can take time. You are on a path to a deeper relationship with him. Just as it takes time to truly get to know someone, it will take time for you to get to know the Holy Spirit. But it is time spent investing in eternity.

"My sheep hear my voice, and I know them, and they follow me." John 10:27

"Behold, I stand at the door and knock. If anyone hears my voice and opens the door, I will come in to him and eat with him, and he with me." Revelation 3:20

"How precious to me are your thoughts, O God! How vast is the sum of them! If I would count them, they are more than the sand. I awake, and I am still with you." Psalm 139:17-18

2. Write down how you feel in God's presence. What senses did you get about his heart? Writing down what God says helps in stewarding what he is so faithful to reveal. You may wish to keep a journal close by to record what God is showing you so you can read back, be reminded and implement what he has spoken.

3. Ask the Holy Spirit to give you the desire, self-control, and faithfulness to spend time each day in his presence developing your relationship with God.

"But the fruit of the Spirit is love, joy, peace, patience, kindness, goodness, faithfulness, gentleness, self-control." Galatians 5:22-23

"You will seek me and find me, when you seek me with all your heart." Jeremiah 29:13

The best way to consistently encounter the transformative love of God is to set aside time early each morning that you'll never miss. Creating a habit can often be difficult. But there is no greater pursuit than a deeper relationship with God. The time you spend with God is of eternal value. Pick a time you can consistently meet with him. Before you go to sleep ask God to give you grace and desire to wake up and encounter him. The more you do it the easier it will become. And as you grow in the knowledge of God and his goodness, time spent with him will become your favorite time of the day. May your day be marked by his transcendent peace and tangible nearness.

Extended Reading: Psalm 139

15

What is worship?

DEVOTIONAL

What is worship through song? When we go to church or gather with other believers, why do we sing? Clearly not everyone finds singing or music to be their greatest passion, so why do we do it?

Worship is first and foremost about the longing of God for unfettered relationship with his people. In authentic worship we can touch the heart of our Creator—satisfying the desires of he who payed the highest price simply to have us. Scripture is clear that God loves when we sing to him and about him. Ephesians 5:18-19 tells us to *"be filled with the Spirit, addressing one another in psalms and hymns and spiritual songs, singing and making melody to the Lord with your heart."* John 4:23 states, *"But the hour is coming, and is now here, when the true worshipers will worship the Father in spirit and truth, for the Father is seeking such people to worship him."*

God loves worship. He longs for it. Think of that! You have an opportunity every day, through worship, to satisfy the heart of the one who paints sunsets, breathes life into dust and forms mountains, galaxies, animals, angels and humankind with just the power of his voice. You bring your Creator immense joy and satisfaction when you worship through singing.

You see, God is after your heart. He's after direct connection from his Spirit to yours. Music has this profound ability to reach past our limited understanding and help our heart connect with he who is limitless and eternal. It serves as an avenue for this cyclical, reciprocal act of love and devotion between the Creator and the created. In worship we discover the reality of God on a level different than reading Scripture or spending time in prayer or community. In worship we can sing to God songs of adoration, thanksgiving, high praise, and unadulterated love in response to his character, nearness, and devotion. Simply put, in worship we give and receive that which is most important—love.

Whether you normally engage in personal worship right now or not, know that you were created to worship. You were made to connect directly with the heart of God. As you engage in the act of worship you will discover the nearness of a God so filled with steadfast love and devotion for you that everything changes. As you consistently touch the heart of the Father your life will be transformed by his limitless grace and passionate pursuit. Engaging in worship will result in an overflowing, unquenchable joy, as there is no greater experience than that of a perfect God meeting with an imperfect person.

Take time in guided prayer to reflect on the importance of worship and connect directly with the heart of your heavenly Father. May your time be marked by a greater revelation of his nearness and love.

GUIDED PRAYER

1. Allow Scripture to fill you with a longing to connect directly with your Creator through worship.

"Make a joyful noise to the Lord, all the earth! Serve the Lord with gladness! Come into his presence with singing! Know that the Lord, he is God! It is he who made us, and we are his; we are his people, and the sheep of his pasture. Enter his gates with thanksgiving, and his courts with praise! Give thanks to him; bless his name!" Psalm 100:1-4

"Oh come, let us sing to the Lord; let us make a joyful noise to the rock of our salvation! Let us come into his presence with thanksgiving; let us make a joyful noise to him with songs of praise! For the Lord is a great God, and a great King above all gods. In his hand are the depths of the earth; the heights of the mountains are his also. The sea is his, for he made it, and his hands formed the dry land. Oh come, let us worship and bow down; let us kneel before the Lord, our Maker!" Psalm 95:1-6

"Ascribe to the Lord the glory due his name; worship the Lord in the splendor of holiness." Psalm 29:2

2. Ask God to show you how much he loves your worship—to give you a revelation of his great love for you. May his desire for worship be the foundation of your devotion.

"But the hour is coming, and is now here, when the true worshipers will worship the Father in spirit and truth, for the Father is seeking such people to worship him." John 4:23

"That you, being rooted and grounded in love, may have strength to comprehend with all the saints what is the breadth and length and height and depth, and to know the love of Christ that surpasses knowledge, that you may be filled with all the fullness of God." Ephesians 3:17-19

"And the four living creatures, each of them with six wings, are full of eyes all around and within, and day and night they never cease to say, 'Holy, holy, holy, is the Lord God Almighty, who was and is and is to come!'" Revelation 4:8

3. Spend some time resting in the presence of God. Ask him to reveal his love to you in a fresh way and worship him in response.

"But for me it is good to be near God." Psalm 73:28

"You make known to me the path of life; in your presence there is fullness of joy; at your right hand are pleasures forevermore." Psalm 16:11

"The Lord your God is in your midst, a mighty one who will save; he will rejoice over you with gladness; he will quiet you by his love; he will exult over you with loud singing." Zephaniah 3:17

If you feel the weight of the world resting on your shoulders at any point today, take a few minutes to engage in worship. A small time of worship has the power to reprioritize our lives and make the stresses and burdens of life diminish in light of God's eternal love. May your day today be marked by the peace and joy of one who knows the love and nearness of the Father.

Extended Reading: John 4

What is a devotional?

DEVOTIONAL

The devotional section of First15 began with the belief that we need our affections for God to be constantly stirred. In the chaos of life, we need a reminder of God's goodness and loving kindness towards us. With all the darkness that surrounds, we need help remembering that God has overcome the world and brought us to the light. This devotional exists to serve that need.

*"So we have come to know and to believe
the love that God has for us. God is love,
and whoever abides in love abides in God,
and God abides in him."*

1 JOHN 4:16

Many wonderful and anointed devotionals line our bookshelves. We can access a seemingly limitless amount of incredible teaching available today. I hope that First15 will faithfully draw you into a daily encounter with the heart of God and fill you with a desire to know him more.

You were created for real, tangible relationship with God. You were created with longings that cannot be satisfied until you experience the fullness of God available to you through the life, death, and resurrection of Jesus. I firmly believe that if you will simply make your heart available to be stirred up by the truth of God's nearness and love, then you will experience whatever it is you've been looking for.

If you will engage with the devotional section of First15 and open your heart that God might speak to you, the Holy Spirit will guide you into an encounter with your omnipotent, omnipresent Creator. God longs to be encountered. He longs for you to know his love. If you will begin each day simply seeking to meet with him for fifteen minutes, your heart will soften and be stirred to live wholly centered around God's goodness.

Encountering God leads to life transformation. Trivial things that seemed to matter before will no longer matter. That which robbed you of joy, purpose and abundant life will no longer have a hold on you. God's love is powerful and real. His desire is for you. His presence is available to you. Take the next few minutes to open your heart and receive a transforming knowledge of God's love.

GUIDED PRAYER

1. Reflect on the depth of God's love for you. Allow Scripture to stir up your desire for God as you meditate on his word.

"No, in all these things we are more than conquerors through him who loved us. For I am sure that neither death nor life, nor angels nor rulers, nor things present nor things to come, nor powers, nor height nor depth, nor anything else in all creation, will be able to separate us from the love of God in Christ Jesus our Lord." Romans 8:37-39

"So we have come to know and to believe the love that God has for us. God is love, and whoever abides in love abides in God, and God abides in him." 1 John 4:16

"So that Christ may dwell in your hearts through faith—that you, being rooted and grounded in love, may have strength to comprehend with all the saints what is the breadth and length and height and depth, and to know the love of Christ that surpasses knowledge, that you may be filled with all the fullness of God." Ephesians 3:17-19

2. Ask the Holy Spirit to give you a revelation of his nearness. Quiet your mind and open your heart to receive his presence. If you have questions about God's presence, reflect on these Scriptures.

"Where shall I go from your Spirit? Or where shall I flee from your presence? If I ascend to heaven, you are there! If I make my bed in Sheol, you are there! If I take the wings of the morning and dwell in the uttermost parts of the sea, even there your hand shall lead me, and your right hand shall hold me." Psalm 139:7-10

"You make known to me the path of life; in your presence there is fullness of joy; at your right hand are pleasures forevermore." Psalm 16:11

3. Take a little time to write down how you feel after encountering God's love. Writing down the effects of encountering God will stir up your heart towards his reality and help you seek him more often.

Evelyn Underhill writes, "This is adoration; not a difficult religious exercise, but an attitude of the soul." May all our lives be marked by an attitude of adoration. May we seek to simply love God moment by moment rather than in infrequent bursts. And may experiencing glorious union with the Holy Spirit as afforded us by Jesus' sacrifice be the foundation for all we do, think, and feel. I pray that your day today would be marked by humble, simple adoration of the King of kings and Lord of lords.

Extended Reading: 1 John 4

What is Prayer?

DEVOTIONAL

Prayer is one of the most fulfilling aspects of Christian spirituality. It's time set aside to simply listen to God, to place our lives in his hands, and to pray in response to the desires of his heart. In 1 Thessalonians 5:17 Scripture tells us to "*pray without ceasing.*" In John 14:13-14 Jesus states, "*Whatever you ask in my name, this I will do, that the Father may be glorified in the Son. If you ask me anything in my name, I will do it.*" But perhaps the most important Scripture on prayer is when Jesus taught us to pray in Matthew 6:5-15.

Because First15 is meant to stir your affections for God and lead you to a transformational encounter with him, I won't walk you through an exegesis of verses 9-15. There are numerous resources (one of which I will point out in the extended reading) to assist you in coming to a better understanding of the depth and applications of Jesus' model prayer. However, I want to focus your attention on verses 5-8 and lead you to a broader definition of prayer so that your prayer life would be marked by God's nearness. Let's walk through that text and then apply it as a model we will use daily in First15. In Matthew 6:5-8, Jesus says:

And when you pray, you must not be like the hypocrites. For they love to stand and pray in the synagogues and at the street corners, that they may be seen by others. Truly, I say to you, they have received their reward. But when you pray, go into your room and shut the door and pray to your Father who is in secret. And your Father who sees in secret will reward you. And when you pray, do not heap up empty phrases as the Gentiles do, for they think that they will be

"What am I to do? I will pray with my spirit, but I will pray with my mind also; I will sing praise with my spirit, but I will sing with my mind also."

1 CORINTHIANS 14:15

heard for their many words. Do not be like them, for your Father knows what you need before you ask him.

First, Jesus teaches us that we are to pray in secret. What an amazing God we have that he desires to meet with us in secret! All of us have a longing to know our Creator in a way that no one else is allowed into. We each need a secret place with our Maker. It's vital to our relationship with God that we set aside time to listen to him and talk with him one on one. It's in this secret place that our relationship with him will go deeper and our lives will be radically transformed.

Next Jesus teaches not to *"heap up empty phrases"* just to be heard for our "many words." Jesus makes it clear that prayer is more about relationship with the Father than the words we say. Prayer is more about the heart than the lips. It's about opening our hearts to God and letting him show us his plan for transformation in both our lives and in the world around us. Mother Theresa said, "Prayer is not asking. Prayer is putting oneself in the hands of God, at His disposition, and listening to His voice in the depth of our hearts." C. S. Lewis wrote, "I don't pray to change God. I pray because I have to. I pray because I can't help myself. It doesn't change God. It changes me."

Do you need God today? Do you need his presence in your life? Do you need to be changed through an encounter with your heavenly Father? Take time in guided prayer to "place [yourself] in the hands of God" and allow him to change you by his goodness and love.

GUIDED PRAYER

1. Take a moment to place yourself "in the hands of God." Open your heart to God and surrender your life to him that all of you would be completely his.

":Arise, and go down to the potter's house, and there I will let you hear my words.' So I went down to the potter's house, and there he was working at his wheel. And the vessel he was making of clay was spoiled in the potter's hand, and he reworked it into another vessel, as it seemed good to the potter to do. Then the word of the Lord came to me: 'O house of Israel, can I not do with you as this potter has done? declares the Lord. Behold, like the clay in the potter's hand, so are you in my hand, O house of Israel.'" Jeremiah 18:2-6

2. Take some time to listen to God. Ask him to lay something on your heart that he wants to accomplish in prayer today. It could be prayer for yourself, for someone you know, or for the nation in which you live. Sometimes God speaks with words, sometimes an inclination or a thought. Pay attention to anything the Spirit lays on your heart and trust his leading.

"My son, if you receive my words and treasure up my commandments with you, making your ear attentive to wisdom and inclining your heart to understanding; yes, if you call out for insight and raise your voice for understanding, if you seek it like silver and search for it as for hidden treasures, then you will understand the fear of the Lord and find the knowledge of God." Proverbs 2:1-5

"Behold, I stand at the door and knock. If anyone hears my voice and opens the door, I will come in to him and eat with him, and he with me." Revelation 3:20

3. Pray for whatever the Spirit puts on your heart. Ask God how to pray for it. Ask God for his will. Through prayer we align ourselves with the heart of God and agree with what he wants to do in us and in the world around us.

Oftentimes we make prayer far more complex than the Lord ever intended. The weight of change does not rest on our shoulders. God alone heals and transforms. Just as salvation is about receiving the gift Jesus already paid for, prayer is about saying yes to what God already wants to do. We never have to beg him for mercy or compassion. He is a Father filled with grace to a level we will never comprehend. But it's in prayer that we discover the grace God has and open ourselves up to be transformed by it. And through prayer we agree with God's heart for others, that we might co-labor with him in what he longs to see happen in the world around us. May your prayer life be filled with the fullness of God and his powerful love.

Extended Reading: Matthew 6

Communion
with God

DAY 5

DEVOTIONAL

The Christian life is meant to be marked by union with God. By the powerful sacrifice of Jesus, the Holy Spirit now dwells within us—longing to make his nearness known. He longs for his perfect love and peace to be the foundation of everything we do, think, and feel.

Brother Lawrence wrote about a life lived in continual communion with God in the book, *The Practice of the Presence of God*. He said "I cannot imagine how religious persons can live satisfied without the practice

"Abide in me, and I in you. As the branch cannot bear fruit by itself, unless it abides in the vine, neither can you, unless you abide in me. I am the vine; you are the branches. Who ever abides in me and I in him, he it is that bears much fruit, for apart from me you can do nothing."

JOHN 15:4-5

of the presence of GOD. For my part I keep myself retired with Him in the depth of centre of my soul as much as I can; and while I am so with Him I fear nothing; but the least turning from Him is insupportable." The more we grow in our knowledge of the profound union that exists between our spirit and the Holy Spirit, the more we will discover our great need of his tangible, constant presence.

Maybe you are at a place where you don't feel like you really know God. Maybe you know about him but don't know him like a friend. In describing the process of coming to know God, Brother Lawrence wrote, "In order to know God, we must often think of Him; and when we come to love Him, we shall then also think of Him often, for our heart will be with our treasure." An amazing transformation takes place in our hearts as our souls awake to our union with God. His love has the power to ignite us toward a lifestyle of seeking greater communion with him.

In many ways our God is infinitely more knowable than any person. Because God is spirit and now dwells within the hearts of believers, he is perfectly able to reveal himself in deeper, more knowable ways than you have access to with anyone else. He has the ability to reveal his thoughts, feelings, power, love, and will moment by moment and in ways that surpass the miscommunication that language often brings. He speaks straight from his Spirit to yours that you may truly know him to greater depths than anyone else. The question is not can we know God, but are we willing to center our lives around the knowledge of him.

Take time in guided prayer to experience union with God. Ask him to reveal his nearness that you might know him in deeper, more tangible ways. May your day be marked by God's presence and love moment by moment as you seek to walk with him in all you do.

GUIDED PRAYER

1. Meditate on Scripture about God's nearness. Allow the word of God to build up your faith to meet with God.

"Where shall I go from your Spirit? Or where shall I flee from your presence? If I ascend to heaven, you are there! If I make my bed in Sheol, you are there! If I take the wings of the morning and dwell in the uttermost parts of the sea, even there your hand shall lead me, and your right hand shall hold me." Psalm 139:7-10

"Behold, I stand at the door and knock. If anyone hears my voice and opens the door, I will come in to him and eat with him, and he with me." Revelation 3:20

2. Do you live in moment by moment union with God? Is your whole life marked by his nearness? Know that God has the fullness of grace and mercy for you no matter what your relationship with him looks like. He desires that you know his love to greater depths.

3. Ask God to reveal his nearness to you. Take time to simply seek a greater knowledge of him. By seeking his face you will experience everything that comes from union with him.

"Then you will call upon me and come and pray to me, and I will hear you. You will seek me and find me, when you seek me with all your heart. I will be found by you, declares the Lord." Jeremiah 29:12-14

"The Lord is good to those who wait for him, to the soul who seeks him." Lamentations 3:25

"And without faith it is impossible to please him, for whoever would draw near to God must believe that he exists and that he rewards those who seek him."
Hebrews 11:6

Your God is both patient and kind. He longs to be with you so you might know his peace. He longs for the foundation of your life to be his love. Seek his face throughout your day today that your life may be marked by his nearness. Don't settle for an ordinary day, but strive for the fullness of life God has for you. May your life be marked by a moment to moment knowledge of God's nearness and love.

Extended Reading: Jeremiah 29

The Presence of God

DAY 6

DEVOTIONAL

One of the most important pieces of spending time with God is encountering his presence. His presence is meant to be at the core of all that we do. God so hated separation from us that Jesus was sent to pay the ultimate price. And at Jesus's death the curtain separating the Holy of Holies from mankind was torn in two—signifying that God's presence was no longer contained but made available to everyone.

"Where shall I go from your Spirit? Or where shall I flee from your presence?"

Psalm 139:7-8 says, *"Where shall I go from your Spirit? Or where shall I flee from your presence? If I ascend to heaven, you are there! If I make my bed in Sheol, you are there!"* And Psalm 84:3-4 says, *"Even the sparrow finds a home, and the swallow a nest for herself, where she may lay her young, at your altars, O LORD of hosts, my King and my God. Blessed are those who dwell in your house, ever singing your praise!"* God's presence is everywhere. There is nowhere you could go that he won't be with you. There is no situation, conversation, job or place in which you can't meet with God.

So how do we encounter the presence of God? How do we experience his nearness? Encountering God is similar to encountering another person. I don't seek an experience with a friend; I simply seek to know him by spending time with him and gain an experience as a result. I don't seek to hear the voice of a friend;

I simply engage in conversation with him as an act of wanting to know him and hear his voice as a result. The only thing about seeking God that makes it different is that he is spirit rather than flesh. John 4:24 says, *"God is spirit, and those who worship him must worship in spirit and truth."* But it's for that very reason that we can truly know him! Scripture is clear that God is everywhere and that the Holy Spirit dwells within us. His presence is already with you. Encountering him is as simple as taking some time to become aware of his nearness.

God longs for you to know him. So great is his desire to meet with you Spirit to spirit, heart to heart, that Jesus gave his life. Take time to simply seek God. Meditate on his word. Allow Scripture to fill your heart with faith. And make space to rest in God's presence that your heart might come alive at the revelation of his nearness.

GUIDED PRAYER

1. Meditate on Scripture about God's presence.

"You make known to me the path of life; in your presence there is fullness of joy; at your right hand are pleasures forevermore" Psalm 16:11

"Where shall I go from your Spirit? Or where shall I flee from your presence? If I ascend to heaven, you are there! If I make my bed in Sheol, you are there! If I take the wings of the morning and dwell in the uttermost parts of the sea, even there your hand shall lead me, and your right hand shall hold me." Psalm 139:7-10

"And he said, 'My presence will go with you, and I will give you rest.'" Exodus 33:14

2. Allow Scripture to fill you with faith to encounter God. Center your understanding of encountering God around simply seeking to know him.

"So faith comes from hearing, and hearing through the word of Christ." Romans 10:17

"And without faith it is impossible to please him, for whoever would draw near to God must believe that he exists and that he rewards those who seek him." Hebrews 11:6

"Trust in the Lord with all your heart, and do not lean on your own understanding. In all your ways acknowledge him, and he will make straight your paths." Proverbs 3:5-6

3. Make space to rest in God's presence. Ask him

to show you how to abide in him. He desires to make himself known to you all throughout your day. He wants to be involved in everything you are doing! Nothing is too mundane for the Lord! His desire is to be with you.

"Draw near to God, and he will draw near to you." James 4:8

"Abide in me, and I in you." John 15:4

"So we have come to know and to believe the love that God has for us. God is love, and whoever abides in love abides in God, and God abides in him." 1 John 4:16

Once you begin consistently encountering God's presence you will find it becomes easier and easier to set aside that time to meet with him. So many Christians are calling the time they spend reading the Bible "time they spend with God," without actually encountering him. We preach as Christians that Jesus is alive; our faith hinges on that fact. Yet we go so long without encountering our God who is alive and present. If we're not regularly encountering the God we serve, we are living and preaching a false gospel by our actions. God's presence is meant to be encountered. He is present, near, active, and full of love for you. May your time spent with him be marked by his satisfying presence as you experience the transforming power of encountering the living God every day.

Extended Reading: Psalm 16

What is Christian Meditation?

DEVOTIONAL

For many years I believed the word of God was meant just for reading and studying—like a textbook on life. I believed it was authored by a good God, and I tried to read it, as I knew I should, but it never made an impact on my life to the level God desired. It wasn't until I discovered the practice of meditation that my life began to be transformed by the powerful, applicable truth of Scripture.

"Blessed is the man [whose]...delight is in the law of the Lord, and on his law he meditates day and night. He is like a tree planted by streams of water that yields fruit in its season, and its leaf does not wither."

PSALM 1:1-3

For many of us the idea of meditation is a confusing one. Modern Christians, notably Protestants, seem to have lost the practice of this important spiritual discipline. We confuse it with practices of other religions, such as Buddhism, and therefore cast it aside as too mystical or even wrong. But Christian meditation does not involve emptying your mind as in Eastern religions; rather it fills us with the knowledge of God and his presence. Meditation is about receiving, not casting out.

So what does meditation look like in the Christian context? To meditate is simply to spend time mulling over a verse, phase, idea or characteristic of God. It's a process where we open up our hearts and minds to receive revelation from the Holy Spirit. To meditate on Scripture is to take a phrase such as *"The Lord is my shepherd; I shall not want,"* and really take time to think about all it means for us personally. For the Lord to be your shepherd means that he will lead you perfectly and lovingly to everything you need. It means that you will not want for what you need in this life. So in the process of meditating you can apply this attribute of God to your present circumstances that you might experience transcendent peace in all situations.

Psalm 1:3 promises that if you meditate on Scripture you will be *"like a tree planted by streams of water that yields fruit in its season, and its leaf does not wither."* Scripture has the power to securely ground you in the steadfast love of your heavenly Father. Hebrews 4:12 says, *"For the word of God is living and active, sharper than any two-edged sword, piercing to the division of soul and of spirit, of joints and of marrow, and discerning the thoughts and intentions of the heart."* Root yourself in the word of God, and watch as your life is filled with the fullness of God. Allow Scripture to be an avenue by which you daily meet with its Author. May your time spent meditating on God's word in guided prayer be marked by his nearness.

GUIDED PRAYER

1. Take a few minutes to meditate on Psalm 1:1-3.
Break it up into little pieces that seem to grab you.

"Blessed is the man who walks not in the counsel of the wicked, nor stands in the way of sinners, nor sits in the seat of scoffers; but his delight is in the law of the Lord, and on his law he meditates day and night. He is like a tree planted by streams of water that yields its fruit in its season, and its leaf does not wither. In all that he does, he prospers." Psalm 1:1-3

2. Take time to reflect on the parts of Psalm 1:1-3 that grab you. Allow the Holy Spirit to give you revelation on how his word can affect your life today.

3. Take time to reflect on what Psalm 1:1-3 says about your heavenly Father. Think about how God gave you his word that you might prosper and bear fruit. Think about his goodness and provision. Allow his character to stir up your affections for him.

The joy of Scripture is that its Author is alive, active and dwells within you. You have direct access to the Holy Spirit who inspired every word of the Bible, and he longs to give you revelation. God longs for his word to not just fill you with knowledge but to dwell in your heart. He longs to use it to lead and guide you into an abundant life filled with love and joy. But you must make time to meditate on it. You must make space in your day to allow Scripture to impact every facet of your life. You must open your heart to God's word as your source of truth so it can transform you. May you be planted by the living water of God's nearness today and bear the fruits of joy and peace in light of God's love.

Extended Reading: Psalm 1

Why spend time alone with God?

"In this the love of God was made manifest among us, that God sent his only Son into the world, so that we might live through him." 1 John 4:19

WEEKLY OVERVIEW

Why should we spend time alone with God? Why is meeting with God in the secret place so important? Until we gain an understanding of the immense value and availability of encountering God, we will never consistently engage in this foundational, vital practice. As we discover God's heart to meet with us in order that we might experience the depths of his love, I pray that your life would be marked by a new grace to consistently and powerfully encounter the living God.

Start Your Day with the Best Thing

DAY 8

DEVOTIONAL

As Christians we know we are supposed to start our day off with God. If you have been a believer for any length of time, you have likely been encouraged by a pastor, teacher, mentor or friend to spend time every morning in God's presence. However, many of us have never been told why God wants us to spend time with him in the morning. We've never discovered all God longs to do in the first moments of our days. We just carry the weight of knowing we should spend time alone with God. We spent last week in First15 going over how to practically spend time with God. This week we're going to talk about the why. Why should you spend time with God every morning?

God longs for your day to begin with the absolute best thing, and the best thing is his presence. If encountering God's presence is the best part of your day, then you already know the impact it has made

"Oh, how abundant is your goodness, which
you have stored up for those who fear you."

PSALM 31:19

on you. I'm glad you're using the tool of First15 as a part of encountering him, and you are incredibly welcome here. For most of us though, I am going to bet that we've yet to fully discover how great spending time with God is. Take a look at your life. How often do you spend time with God? This isn't a report card where the people with the most consistent quiet times get a gold star. Be real with yourself. This is for your benefit. Take a moment and assess how often you actually spend time meeting with God.

You see, we will only ever consistently do that which we want to do, especially with our free time. We might have to go to work. We might feel obligated to people or practices. But with our personal time, our wants will always win out over our obligations. For many years I tried to spend time with God out of obligation. As a result, I hardly ever did it. It wasn't until I encountered the incredible love and peace inherent in God's presence that I began to actually desire to spend time with him. Once I felt the satisfaction only his presence can bring, I began to crave time with him out of a need to satisfy my longings for love, purpose, and relationship. I discovered that my time spent with God was the absolute best part of my day.

Psalm 16:11 says, *"You make known to me the path of life; in your presence there is fullness of joy; at your right hand are pleasures forevermore."* And Psalm 84:1-2 says, *"How lovely is your dwelling place, O Lord of hosts! My soul longs, yes, faints for the courts of the Lord; my heart and flesh sing for joy to the living God."* I can attest that consistently receiving a revelation of God's love has been the single most transformative part of my life. The days I don't start with the best thing, being in his presence, are my worst days by far. His presence ignites me with passion, love, purpose, and a sense of belonging that nothing else can give.

Wherever you are in relation to God today, do you want to know him more? Do you want a deeper revelation of his goodness and love? Take time to open your heart to God and allow him to satisfy your eternal need for communion with the Father. Allow him to fill you with his presence that you might experience the reality of his love. And let a true, transformative encounter with the living God fill you with a greater hunger to consistently encounter God in the first moments of each day.

May your time spent today encountering God in guided prayer be filled with the *"fullness of joy"* (Psalm 16:11).

47

GUIDED PRAYER

1. Take some time to receive God's presence. Meditate on the truth of Scripture and allow God to reveal the reality of his nearness.

"Oh, how abundant is your goodness, which you have stored up for those who fear you." Psalm 31:19

"You make known to me the path of life; in your presence there is fullness of joy; at your right hand are pleasures forevermore." Psalm 16:11

"How lovely is your dwelling place, O Lord of hosts! My soul longs, yes, faints for the courts of the Lord; my heart and flesh sing for joy to the living God." Psalm 84:1-2

2. Assess your own heart. How consistently do you spend time with God? Do you feel like spending time with him is in any way an obligation rather than a desire? Be honest with God! He longs to pour out his limitless grace over anything that is holding you back from experiencing the fullness of his love.

3. Ask God to reveal his desire to meet with you. Ask him how he feels about you. Ask him to reveal the desires of your heart that he longs to satisfy in spending time alone with him. Journal anything he shows you.

Before you go to bed tonight take a minute to get in God's presence. Let his goodness be the last thing you think of before you go to sleep and the first thing you wake up to in the morning. Throughout the day, if you feel down, passionless, or weary, take a minute to reflect on the goodness of God. He longs to spend time with you throughout your day, filling you with joy, passion, and purpose for bringing his kingdom to earth in all you do. May your day be filled with the fullness of God today.

Extended Reading: Psalm 84

49

Storing the Treasure of Your Heart in Heaven

DAY 9

DEVOTIONAL

In Matthew 6:19-21 Jesus teaches us an important spiritual principle we need to know in order to give God the entirety of our hearts. Scripture says:

Do not lay up for yourselves treasures on earth, where moth and rust destroy and where thieves break in and steal, but lay up for yourselves treasures in heaven, where neither moth nor rust destroys and where thieves do not break in and steal. For where your treasure is, there your heart will be also.

You are the child of a loving God who is desperately jealous for the entirety of your heart. Matthew 6:19-21 illustrates a truth that spans beyond this world and into the fullness of eternity. You and I have an opportunity in this life either to give our hearts to God and receive an eternal reward, or to give our hearts to the world, which will only lead to destruction. We can either surrender all that we are and have to the perfect, pleasing plans of our heavenly Father or seek fulfillment, pleasure, status, and wealth in that which belongs to the world alone.

The absolute best way we can ensure our lives are fully surrendered and available to the Father is to

> *"Do not lay up for yourselves treasures on earth, where moth and rust destroy and where thieves break in and steal, but lay up for yourselves treasures in heaven, where neither moth nor rust destroys and where thieves do not break in and steal. For where your treasure is, there your heart will be also."*

MATTHEW 6:19-21

spend the first moments of our day alone with him. If we are going to make the most of this life, we must set aside time to assess our thoughts, actions, and emotions. We must make time to take an honest look at our lives and discover whether we are truly living for God or for the world. And in response to a daily assessment, we must consistently engage in the process of confession so that our lives may be empowered by the forgiveness and love of the Father.

God longs for your life here on earth to impact eternity. He is a Father who has perfect plans to bless you in ways you cannot imagine. But God cannot bless that which is not best. He cannot reward you for doing that which is destructive. Choose to center your life around meeting with God that you might store up a wealth of eternal treasure. Open your heart to the Holy Spirit every morning that he may reveal anything that's keeping you from experiencing the fullness of life Jesus died to give you. Surrender your life to the God who has greater things in store for you than you can ask or imagine. And experience the peace and joy that comes from allowing God to have the entirety of your life to bless and fill with his glorious nearness.

GUIDED PRAYER

1. Meditate on the truth of God's word. Allow Scripture to fill you with a desire to surrender your life fully to God's plans and love.

"Do not lay up for yourselves treasures on earth, where moth and rust destroy and where thieves break in and steal, but lay up for yourselves treasures in heaven, where neither moth nor rust destroys and where thieves do not break in and steal. For where your treasure is, there your heart will be also."

2. In what ways are you laying up treasure on earth? Where are you seeking fulfillment and provision from the world rather than God? What parts of your life are not God's best for you?

3. Confess any sin in your life to God and take time to receive his forgiveness. God hates sin because it robs us of the fullness of life he longs to give. Once we confess our sins to him he truly forgives us. Don't dwell on your sin, but rather on

"If we confess our sins, he is faithful and just to forgive us our sins and to cleanse us from all unrighteousness." 1 John 1:9

Oswald Chambers wrote, "Joy means the perfect fulfilment of that for which I was created and regenerated." You were created and regenerated for unhindered communion with your heavenly Father. Experiencing true joy in this life will be the result of casting aside anything that chains your heart to this world. Live today for God alone and discover the wealth of life that comes from storing up your treasure in heaven.

Extended Reading: Ephesians 1

Live for Love

DEVOTIONAL

If there is one major theme in the narrative of Scripture it's the power of God's love. It was his love that caused our creation. It was in love that he offered mankind grace even in our continual rebellion. It was his love that sent Jesus to rescue us, and it's his love that will win at our final redemption—the gathering of all of God's people for the great wedding feast.

God is love. He can do nothing apart from love. Jesus says in Mark 12:30-31 that all of the commandments are summed up for us in one word—love. You were created to be loved by God and to love him and others in return. And you will never find satisfaction until you rest in the unconditional love of your heavenly Father. You will never find true purpose until you live to love God and others.

> *"'And you shall love the Lord your God with all your heart and with all your soul and with all your mind and with all your strength.' The second is this: 'You shall love your neighbor as yourself.' There is no other commandment greater than these."*

MARK 12:30-31

To live for love is to step outside of the ways and cares of this world and live for the kingdom of God. It's to choose to root yourself in the unconditional affection of your heavenly Father rather than seeking fulfillment from the fickle love of mankind. It's to choose to serve and give rather than looking to receive from a world that has so little to offer. To live for love is to seek first God and his ways and thereby receive the fullness of life only he can give.

When you begin your days in the presence of God, you lay for yourself a foundation of God's unconditional love. To allow God to invade the first moments of your day with the truth of his love for you will strengthen you to stop looking for fulfillment in the things of the world. It is impossible to live for love as Jesus commands unless we first receive daily the perfect, powerful love of our heavenly Father. *"We love because he first loved us"* (1 John 4:19).

My hope and prayer is that First15 could be a beneficial resource for you to encounter the love of God. I pray this love fills your heart to overflowing, and then in response to the love of God you advance his kingdom of love on earth. God's love for you is so intense, so purposeful, and so abundant that just a taste of it has the power to shift your life from one lived selfishly to one lived sacrificially. May his love stir your affections for him and others. May you live a life transformed by the love of your heavenly Father today. May you live for love.

GUIDED PRAYER

1. Receive God's presence. Take time to focus on his nearness, on how it changes your outlook and emotions. Spend the majority of your prayer time today on this point, just being overwhelmed by the depth of God's love.

"So we have come to know and to believe the love that God has for us. God is love, and whoever abides in love abides in God, and God abides in him." 1 John 4:16

"Where shall I go from your Spirit? Or where shall I flee from your presence?" Psalm 139:7

2. Give God your affections in return. Tell him you love him. Tell him you love how he makes you feel. Thank him for the work he is doing in your life.

3. Ask God to help you live for others. Ask him to show you where he is working in the lives of those around you. Ask him to reveal how he would have you partner with him today in advancing his kingdom.

"I am the vine; you are the branches. Whoever abides in me and I in him, he it is that bears much fruit, for apart from me you can do nothing." John 15:5

"This is my commandment, that you love one another as I have loved you. Greater love has no one than this, that someone lay down his life for his friends. You are my friends if you do what I command you." John 15:12-14

"For we are his workmanship, created in Christ Jesus for good works, which God prepared beforehand, that we should walk in them." Ephesians 2:10

Take a moment to read Ephesians 3:16-19, which so perfectly sums up the power and reality of love:

That according to the riches of his glory he may grant you to be strengthened with power through his Spirit in your inner being, so that Christ may dwell in your hearts through faith—that you, being rooted and grounded in love, may have strength to comprehend with all the saints what is the breadth and length and height and depth, and to know the love of Christ that surpasses knowledge, that you may be filled with all the fullness of God.

Extended Reading: 1 John 3

Renewing Your Mind

DAY 11

DEVOTIONAL

Your mind is the battleground on which the war for your emotions, purpose, effectiveness, and fullness of life is won or lost. It's your mind that is attacked daily by the enemy. It's your mind that the world is trying to influence for its own benefit. And it's your mind that the Lord desires to renew daily in order for you to live in abundant relationship with him. So if the mind truly is a battleground, how do you come out the winner? How do you come out victorious over Satan and his schemes?

Scripture says clearly that to achieve victory over your mind it must be continually renewed by the power of God's word. Romans 12:2 states *"Do not be conformed to this world, but be transformed by the renewal of your mind, that by testing you may discern what is the will of God, what is good and acceptable and perfect."* God puts conforming to the world and being transformed by the renewal of your mind in opposition. There is no grey area. Your mind is either being won for the kingdom of God or lost to the world. You are either thinking pleasing thoughts to God or not. You are either experiencing the abundant life Jesus made available to you or not.

For a long time, the idea of renewing my mind felt exhausting. Honestly, reading the Bible was incredibly boring for me. But I discovered that the Bible is only as life-giving to me as I am willing to be transformed by it. Until we actually sit down, open our hearts, and allow ourselves to be transformed by God's word, we will never experience the life that comes from

"Finally, brothers, whatever is true, whatever is honorable, whatever is just, whatever is pure, whatever is lovely, whatever is commendable, if there is any excellence, if there is anything worthy of praise, think about these things."

PHILIPPIANS 4:8

victory in our minds. The thoughts that plague you—the thoughts that rob you of freedom, peace, and joy—will never leave you until you allow your mind to be renewed by God's word.

To ignore the war being waged around us is to lose the war. Our enemy longs for us to become complacent against his attacks. He longs for us to believe sinful thoughts, wrongful attitudes and lies are just a part of life on earth. He knows he has no power against the ability of God's word to transform us.

So, how do you renew your mind? Philippians 4:8 says *"Finally, brothers, whatever is true, whatever is honorable, whatever is just, whatever is pure, whatever is lovely, whatever is commendable, if there is any excellence, if there is anything worthy of praise, think about these things."* Set your thoughts on the things of God. Begin every day by setting your mind on the wonderful character of the living God and your new identity in Christ. If you will allow God's word to be the foundation of your thought life by spending your first moments meditating on Scripture, the battle for your mind will be won for the kingdom. The negative thoughts and insecurities you face daily will flee from you in the glorious light of God's truth. That's God's promise for you today and every day.

Take time today to meditate on Scripture and experience the transformative power of grace over your thoughts as you enter into guided prayer.

GUIDED PRAYER

1. Meditate on 2 Corinthians 5:17.

"Therefore, if anyone is in Christ, he is a new creation. The old has passed away; behold, the new has come." 2 Corinthians 5:17

Repeat it over and over again, even out loud. Put yourself in the Scripture. Declare over yourself, "I am in Christ and a new creation. The old, sinful me has passed away, and the new me in Christ has come." Allow the truth of Scripture to impact the way you see yourself and your world.

2. In what way do your thoughts or life not line up with the truth of 2 Corinthians 5:17? In what ways do you see yourself as anything but a new creation? In what ways do you identify with your sin rather than the freedom afforded you by the blood of Jesus?

3. Journal what God shows you. Take these areas of your life and submit them to the truth of Scripture. Ask the Holy Spirit to help you see yourself as he sees you. Allow your perspectives to be changed by the Lord in order to see yourself as he does.

God's word is truer than how you feel, and if you will align your life with the truth of Scripture it will begin to powerfully affect your emotions. Emotions are the result of the way we think. We feel loved because we believe we are loved. We feel joy because we believe there is cause for joy. In the same way, when we believe a lie from the enemy our emotions are powerfully impacted. When we believe we'll never get victory over a sin, that no one loves us, or that we're not good enough, our lives begin to bear the fruit of those lies. But there is power when we root ourselves in the word of God. Transcendent joy and peace come when we establish God's word as our basis for truth. May your day be marked by a new freedom as the result of renewing your mind.

Extended Reading: Colossians 3:1-17

Having Time Alone

DEVOTIONAL

Why is time alone with God so important? Why can't just going to church, a community group, or a Bible study be enough? Those of us who have grown up in church or have been going to church for many years have been told that time spent alone with God is vital to our relationship with him. Many of us, however, were never given a reason why. And in order for us to consistently and effectively engage in this crucial practice, we must understand why it is so important.

Here's what we learn from Scripture about having time alone with God. Scripture makes it abundantly clear that Jesus spent time alone with his heavenly Father. Luke 5:16 states, *"Jesus often withdrew to lonely places and prayed."* Mark 1:35 states, *"And rising very early in the morning, while it was still dark, he departed and went out to a desolate place, and there he prayed."* Often in Scripture, Jesus withdrew from the crowd to pray. So the first reason to spend time alone with God is because Jesus did. If Jesus needed

*"Jesus often withdrew to
lonely places and prayed."*

LUKE 5:16

time alone with his heavenly Father, we can all be sure we need it even more. Jesus walked in God's presence constantly. Jesus constantly responded to God's will for his life. He is our perfect example. And even still, he needed time alone with God.

We also see from Jesus' example that time alone with God empowers us to carry out God's purpose for our life. It was after withdrawing into the wilderness in Luke 4 that he began performing miracles. Jesus entered the Garden of Gethsemane filled with grief and sorrow, asking God for a way other than his own death to achieve salvation for his people. After spending time alone with God, he came out of the garden empowered to endure the worst atrocity in history. Spending time alone with God empowers us to live a life filled with a knowledge of God's purposes and the ability to faithfully see them through.

Lastly, Jesus is clear in Matthew 6:5-6 how we are to pray. Scripture says, *"And when you pray, you must*

not be like the hypocrites. For they love to stand and pray in the synagogues and at the street corners, that they may be seen by others. Truly, I say to you, they have received their reward. But when you pray, go into your room and shut the door and pray to your Father who is in secret. And your Father who sees in secret will reward you." God rewards time spent alone with him in prayer. It's by praying in secret that we clearly and tangibly encounter God's love for us. It's by spending time engaging in conversation with the Spirit that we learn what his voice sounds like. It's by asking God questions that we discover his will. And it's by spending time alone with him that our lives become centered around his nearness and goodness.

All of the money in the world cannot buy the rewards God longs to give you. All the favor of men will not satisfy your insatiable desire to be fully known and fully loved. Receive right now the best gift you could be offered, one-on-one communion with your heavenly Father.

GUIDED PRAYER

1. Wherever you are, find a place to get alone and pray. Seek out a place that you can find solitude that will be uninterrupted.

"Jesus often withdrew to lonely places and prayed."
Luke 5:16

"And rising very early in the morning, while it was still dark, he departed and went out to a desolate place, and there he prayed." Mark 1:35

2. Read and pray through this Scripture. May God give you a revelation of his provision and love for you as you pray Jesus's model prayer.

"Our Father in heaven,
hallowed be your name.
Your kingdom come,
your will be done,
on earth as it is in heaven.
Give us this day our daily bread,
and forgive us our debts,
as we also have forgiven our debtors.
And lead us not into temptation,
but deliver us from evil."
Matthew 6:9-13

3. Engage in conversation with God. Ask him how he feels about you. Come before him with anything that is weighing you down and lay your burdens at his feet. Rest in the peace that comes from his presence.

"Come to me, all who labor and are heavy laden, and I will give you rest. Take my yoke upon you, and learn from me, for I am gentle and lowly in heart, and you will find rest for your souls. For my yoke is easy, and my burden is light."
Matthew 11:28-30

God's desire to spend time alone with you is not meant to add stress or pressure to your life but to relieve you from it. He is not a God who is after you religiously checking off a quiet time box, but a good Father who longs to fill your life with his grace, power, and love. Spend some time today mulling over these important questions from Brennan Manning written in his book, *The Furious Longing of God*. May your day be marked by the love of your kind, good Father.

"Is your own personal prayer life characterized by the simplicity, childlike candor, boundless trust, and easy familiarity of a little one crawling up in Daddy's lap? An assured knowing that the daddy doesn't care if the child falls asleep, starts playing with toys, or even starts chatting with little friends, because the daddy knows the child has essentially chosen to be with him for that moment? Is that the spirit of your interior prayer life?"

Extended Reading: Matthew 6

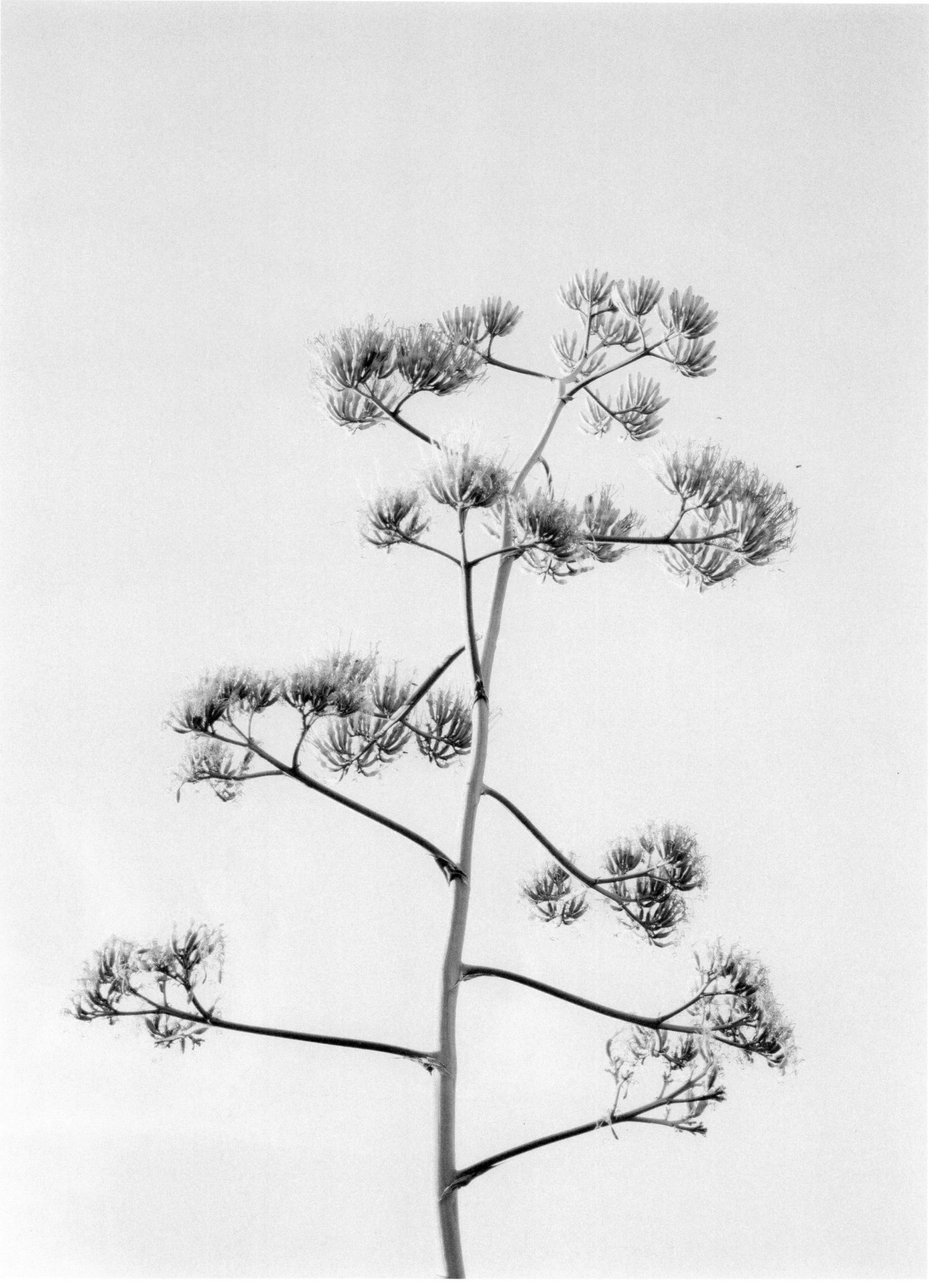

Life in Surrender

DEVOTIONAL

There is a life available to us as believers that few find—a life free from burden, fear, boredom, and emptiness. The problem is that the road to life requires a complete sacrifice of ourselves. The road to purpose, passion, joy and freedom requires that we die to ourselves every hour of every day. Jesus made the way to freedom open and clear for us. Scripture serves as the perfect practical handbook to walk that narrow road. And the Holy Spirit serves

"Enter by the narrow gate. For the gate is wide and the way is easy that leads to destruction, and those who enter by it are many. For the gate is narrow and the way is hard that leads to life, and those who find it are few."

MATTHEW 7:13-14

as the perfect guide and friend along the way. We have everything we need available to us;, however, most of us lack a willingness to sacrifice fully so that the seeds of our surrender lead to the fruition of an abundant life.

Jesus charges us to lose our lives in order to gain life with God. In Matthew 10:39 he says, *"Whoever finds his life will lose it, and whoever loses his life for my sake will find it."* The only way for you to truly find abundant life in God is to surrender your life for his sake. In fact, all of creation testifies to this truth. Think for a second of those trying to find their lives on their own instead of in God. Humans have an insatiable lust for affection, purpose, security, and love. No matter how loved a person is by society, it's never enough. No matter how much money a person makes, they could always make a little more. No matter how driven a person is, there is always more they could be doing. We are lost without God.

Seeing these people makes me evaluate my own life and search for areas I haven't surrendered to God yet. Thinking about their insatiable lust for more makes me look for my own. I *need* my life to have purpose. I *need* to be loved, to have freedom,

and to feel satisfied. I experience satisfaction only inasmuch as I have surrendered my life to God. God will not fill what is closed off to him. He does not force his will upon us. Rather, he waits patiently, quietly beckoning us to lose our lives so that he can lavish on us a life greater and more filled with his goodness than we could have ever imagined.

Our Father longs for us to be loved completely. He longs for us to be completely secure by trusting him. He longs for us to be fully satisfied. Will you answer his beckoning today? Will you choose to trust him? He is so faithful—more faithful than you will ever fully know. You cannot count all the ways in which he desires to love you. The immense depth of his love is bottomless. But will you spend your life trying to search it out? Proverbs 25:2 says *"It is the glory of God to conceal things, but the glory of kings is to search things out."* Will you search out the depths of God's love today? Will you make as much room in your heart as possible for him to come dwell? Will you lose your life today so that you may find it in him? The road is narrow. It will take work. It will take sacrifice. It will take everything. But you will gain immeasurably more in return.

Listen to the Spirit today as you enter into guided prayer and respond in whatever ways he leads you.

67

GUIDED PRAYER

1. Take a minute to quiet your heart and mind.
Open your hands as a sign of being ready to receive anything God would show you.

"The Lord your God is in your midst, a mighty one who will save; he will rejoice over you with gladness; he will quiet you by his love; he will exult over you with loud singing." Zephaniah 3:17

2. Ask the Lord to show you anything in your life that isn't in his will. Pay attention to anything that comes up in your mind. It could be a person, place, thing, habit, recurring thought, etc.

3. Surrender anything in your life that isn't God's will for you. Confess any sin that's holding you back from the fullness of life available to you in Jesus. Ask God for wisdom on how to end a relationship or a commitment. Ask him for grace and help to mend any relationships that he desires to heal. Surrender the entirety of your heart that you would be fully his today.

"Humble yourselves, therefore, under the mighty hand of God so that at the proper time he may exalt you, casting all your anxieties on him, because he cares for you." 1 Peter 5:6-7

You can only experience the fruit of the Spirit through things born of the Spirit. God cannot bless sin and selfishness because it isn't good for you. If God were to bless something that wasn't best for you, you would keep doing it! If a dating relationship isn't blessed, if it isn't born of the Spirit, get out of it. If a friend leads you away from God instead of to him, stop hanging out with him or her. If a lifestyle choice you are making doesn't have the peace of God in it, quit doing it. Surrender seems to cost so much at the time, but it will be the best decision you ever make. Set your life on the narrow path God has laid out for you. Live your life in response to the Spirit and to his word. The life you find in God will be immeasurably greater than any life you could find on your own.

Extended Reading: Matthew 7

Freedom through Enjoying God

DEVOTIONAL

You were created to enjoy God. The Westminster shorter catechism says, "Man's chief end is to glorify God and enjoy Him forever." David wrote in Psalm 16:11, *"You make known to me the path of life; in your presence there is fullness of joy; at your right hand are pleasures forevermore."* We were designed to seek enjoyment in God. We were made to delight ourselves

> *"Therefore, if anyone is in Christ, he is a new creation. The old has passed away; behold, the new has come."*

2 CORINTHIANS 5:17

in his goodness, his provision, the wonders of his creation, and the simplicity of his unconditional love. So important—so powerful—is finding enjoyment in God that it has the power to set us free from sin. You see, when we don't seek enjoyment in God we will naturally seek it in the world. We can't live our lives apart from pleasure. We aren't created to live without happiness, love, passion, and joy.

Most of us have been indoctrinated to the idea that we sin because we aren't controlled enough. We believe that if we could just get rid of a need for pleasure or enjoyment, we'd be free. Self-control is absolutely crucial in experiencing freedom from sin, but we will never be able rid ourselves of our immense need to enjoy life. We will never stop seeking pleasure because we were made to be satisfied in the riches of God's love.

Until you establish a daily rhythm of enjoying God, you will never experience true freedom from sin. Until your longing to be fully known and fully loved is satisfied in the wealth of God's affection for you, you will never stop seeking it elsewhere. Until you know beyond a shadow of a doubt that you are cared for, thought about, liked, and wanted by your Creator, you will never stop trying to satisfy those needs in others.

Psalm 34:8 says, *"Oh, taste and see that the Lord is good! Blessed is the man who takes refuge in him!"* Take time today to taste and see that your heavenly Father is truly good. Allow him to fill you with a revelation of his love. Rest in his presence. And as you enjoy God, allow him to draw you deeper in toward his heart and away from the cares and pursuits of the world.

GUIDED PRAYER

1. Reflect on your need for joy and pleasure. Look at your own life and acknowledge your need for passion, purpose, happiness, peace and joy.

2. In what ways are you seeking fulfillment in the world? What sin in your life is the result of not being fully satisfied in God? Who or what are you turning to for fulfillment in opposition to God?

3. Take time to let God to satisfy your longings. Open your heart to God and let him reveal the depths of his love. Ask him for a revelation of how he likes you, wants you, and enjoys you. Let his love for you begin to draw you near.

"Draw near to God, and he will draw near to you." James 4:8

"Oh, taste and see that the Lord is good! Blessed is the man who takes refuge in him!" Psalm 34:8

"You make known to me the path of life; in your presence there is fullness of joy; at your right hand are pleasures forevermore." Psalm 16:11

1 Corinthians 2:9-10 says, *"But, as it is written, 'What no eye has seen, nor ear heard, nor the heart of man imagined, what God has prepared for those who love him'—these things God has revealed to us through the Spirit. For the Spirit searches everything, even the depths of God."* Through the Holy Spirit, you can know how God feels about you. You have access to a limitless wealth of affection and unconditional love. God has unimaginable things prepared for you simply because he loves you. May you find total fulfillment today in the goodness and love of your heavenly Father.

Extended Reading: 2 Corinthians 5

Centering your life around meeting with God

"Behold, I stand at the door and knock. If anyone hears my voice and opens the door, I will come in to him and eat with him, and he with me." Revelation 3:20

WEEKLY OVERVIEW

This life is marked by a single choice: who or what will we center our lives around? This choice takes each of us down a path of decisions that shape who we are, what we feel, who or what we value, and what we will have accomplished at the end of our days. To center our lives around ourselves or the things of this world leads only to destruction. But, to center our lives around meeting with God fills each moment with the glorious abundance of God's love, provision, and transcendent peace. May your life be marked by union with your Creator as we explore what it means to center our lives around meeting with God this week.

Choosing a Center

DEVOTIONAL

What would our lives look like if we truly centered our time, energy, emotions, and pursuits around meeting with God? All of us choose to center our lives around something or someone. Every decision is made through the filter of what we most value. For some of us, we center our lives around ourselves. For others, we center our lives around the opinions of others. Still others choose to center life around a notion or concept, believing it to be of the highest value. My prayer is that we as the body of Christ would begin to center our lives here on earth around meeting with our Creator because he is absolutely the most worthy recipient of our highest value.

"The end of the matter; all has been heard.
Fear God and keep his commandments, for
this is the whole duty of man."

ECCLESIASTES 12:13

To center our lives around meeting with God is to place value on the absolute best thing. Psalm 84:10-12 says, *"For a day in your courts is better than a thousand elsewhere. I would rather be a doorkeeper in the house of my God than dwell in the tents of wickedness. For the Lord God is a sun and shield; the Lord bestows favor and honor. No good thing does he withhold from those who walk uprightly. O Lord of hosts, blessed is the one who trusts in you!"* When we place our trust and value in God, we position ourselves to live in blissful communion with the Father who loves us. Our God longs to meet with us. He longs for us to taste and see his goodness. It's only in living for communion with our Creator above all else that we will experience the incredible, abundant life God longs to give us.

For most of my life I would have told you God was my center. I would have said that Jesus was my highest value. But my actions, time, thoughts, and emotions in no way reflected those statements. You see, we spend time with those we most love. We center our emotions, actions, and thoughts around whatever person or thing we most value. Unless our lives truly reflect a posture of being centered around Jesus, we must take an honest assessment of ourselves and ask God to help us make changes. We must bring our brokenness and sin before God and ask for his perfect help in transforming us into children marked by his presence.

Centering our lives around anything but Jesus will only lead us to disappointment and dissatisfaction. This world has nothing good to offer us. To center our lives around ourselves will only increase the burdens and stresses of this world. To center our lives around people will only lead to an emotional rollercoaster driven by the brokenness and frailty of others. And to center our lives around an idea or concept will only store up treasure as lasting as this already passing world.

Take time today to look honestly at your heart. Allow the Holy Spirit to reveal any ways in which your life isn't centered around meeting with God. Confess any worldly or selfish pursuits and seek to center your life around incredible, boundless communion with your good and loving heavenly Father.

GUIDED PRAYER

1. Meditate on the importance of centering your life around meeting with God. Allow Scripture to stir up your heart to place the highest value in communion with your Creator.

"The Lord is good to those who wait for him, to the soul who seeks him." Lamentations 3:25

"The end of the matter; all has been heard. Fear God and keep his commandments, for this is the whole duty of man." Ecclesiastes 12:13

2. Where is your life not centered around meeting with God? Where have you been placing your value, energy, time, and emotions other than Jesus?

"For am I now seeking the approval of man, or of God? Or am I trying to please man? If I were still trying to please man, I would not be a servant of Christ." Galatians 1:10

3. Ask the Holy Spirit to help you recenter your life today. Ask him to show you what it looks like to truly center your life around meeting with God. Make the decision to value relationship with God above all else.

"For a day in your courts is better than a thousand elsewhere. I would rather be a doorkeeper in the house of my God than dwell in the tents of wickedness. For the Lord God is a sun and shield; the Lord bestows favor and honor. No good thing does he withhold from those who walk uprightly. O Lord of hosts, blessed is the one who trusts in you!" Psalm 84:10-12

"I love those who love me, and those who seek me diligently find me." Proverbs 8:17

To truly center our lives around God is to free ourselves from the constraints of both the world and religion. God does not desire legalism in meeting with him. He is not angry with you for spending time with friends, entertainment, or other things you enjoy. He simply wants to be the chief longing of your heart. He wants to be with you as you spend time with friends, family, entertainment, and anything else your heart desires. Of course he wants you to meet with him in the secret place. Of course he wants you to follow his leadership if he guides you away from something. But as your heart grows to be truly his, you will begin to want the things he wants. You will begin to spend your time as it can best be spent. And you will begin to truly center your life around the goodness you can only find in the presence of your heavenly Father. May your day today be marked by the simplicity and joy of communing with a good, near, and loving God.

Extended Reading: Psalm 84

The Longing of God to Meet with You

DAY 16

DEVOTIONAL

I used to view my time spent in secret with my heavenly Father as something for which I needed to drum up desire. I pictured God waiting for me in a room, ready to bless me for sure, but I felt the weight of choosing him was all on my shoulders. The truth of God's heart is far from my previous misconceptions.

We serve a God who constantly, sweetly, and powerfully pursues us. Revelation 3:20 says, *"Behold, I stand at the door and knock. If anyone hears my voice and opens the door, I will come in to him and eat with him, and he with me."* God is knocking on the door of your heart right now. With every gentle fall breeze that moves sweetly across your face, with every beautiful sunrise, with every breathtaking star in the sky, God is declaring his love for you.

God pursues us in any and every way he can. The greatest desire of his heart is for communion with his people. So it's in knowing and receiving his overwhelming affections for us that our hearts will be stirred to meet with him. It's in taking time to notice his constant pursuit of us that we will naturally begin to center our lives around meeting with our heavenly Father.

You see, the reason we should center our lives around meeting with God is because at the center of his heart is a deep, insatiable longing to meet with us. The Creator of the universe deeply longs to continually, consistently meet with you. God, who is Almighty, all-knowing, filled with grace, and is the fulfillment of perfect love, longs to be known by you. We are created to be drawn by the desire of our Creator. We are made to be known and to know our heavenly Father. We are created to walk with him every moment of every day. It's not that we "should" center our lives around meeting with God, it's that we were created to and must.

Song of Solomon 7:10 says, *"I am my beloved's, and his desire is for me."* May you grow in the awareness of God's desire for you today. May you come to know yourself as *"my beloved's."* May your life be marked by the natural response to your Creator's unending pursuit of you. And may you center your life around meeting with God, not out of obligation, but because he so desperately longs to meet with you.

GUIDED PRAYER

1. Meditate on God's desire to meet with you.

"Behold, I stand at the door and knock. If anyone hears my voice and opens the door, I will come in to him and eat with him, and he with me." Revelation 3:20

"You did not choose me, but I chose you." John 15:16

2. What does it mean for your life that your loving Creator continually pursues you? What would it be like to live a life marked by responding to God's love in every moment?

3. Take time to meet with God. Ask him how he feels about you. Ask him to reveal his desire for you. Respond to his affections with your own. Tell him honestly how you feel.

"I am my beloved's, and his desire is for me." Song of Solomon 7:10

"How precious to me are your thoughts, O God! How vast is the sum of them! If I would count them, they are more than the sand. I awake, and I am still with you." Psalm 139:17-18

All you have is today. Centering your life around meeting with God is all about the choices you make today. The way you choose to live right now will impact your days to come. Don't worry about your track record. Don't concern yourself with the idea of meeting with Jesus every day for the rest of your life. Simply choose to enjoy him today. *"Sufficient for the day is its own trouble"* (Matthew 6:34).

Extended Reading: Psalm 139

Seeing God as Our Father

DEVOTIONAL

If there's one name for God that has the power to dramatically transform the lives of believers, it's that we can call God "Abba" or "Father." To see God as our Father changes everything. As we read a few days ago, in Brennan Manning's book, *The Furious Longing of God*, he asks a pertinent and powerful question:

Is your own personal prayer life characterized by the simplicity, childlike candor, boundless trust, and easy familiarity of a little one crawling up in Daddy's lap? An assured knowing that the daddy doesn't care if the child falls asleep, starts playing with

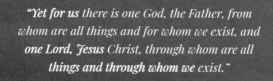

"Yet for us there is one God, the Father, from whom are all things and for whom we exist, and one Lord, Jesus Christ, through whom are all things and through whom we exist."

1 CORINTHIANS 8:6

toys, or even starts chatting with little friends, because the daddy knows the child has essentially chosen to be with him for that moment? Is that the spirit of your interior prayer life?

When I first read these questions I thought to myself, "Surely it can't be this simple. Surely this can't be all God expects of me." We've missed the mark on what it truly means to be children of a good, near, and loving Father. We've projected our own insecurities, perspectives, and experiences on a God who is love embodied. There is nothing we can ever do to make God love us any more than he already does. And there is nothing we can ever do to make him love us any less. God loves us because he loves us. He enjoys us because he enjoys us. He wants to be with us because that's how he is, not because we somehow earn his desire for us.

John 3:16 says, *"For God so loved the world, that he gave his only Son, that whoever believes in him should not perish but have eternal life."* Even while we were in sin and separation from God, he loved us enough to pay the highest price to have us. So great was his depth of love for us that Jesus laid down his own life as the atonement for our mistakes, failures, weaknesses, and frailty. If God loved us then unconditionally, he loves us now unconditionally. If God would choose us then, he chooses us now. If God desired us then, he desires us now.

If we're going to center our lives around meeting with God, we must understand the nature of his love for us. We must begin to relate to him as our good and loving Father above all else. We must cast aside any notion that he is angry with us, far from us, or void of affection or desire for us. We will only be drawn to our heavenly Father to the degree that we take him at his word and trust in his love for us. Take time today to receive the overwhelming, unconditional love of God for you. Allow his love to reorient your perspectives and beliefs. And respond to his great love by opening your heart and having fellowship with your Creator, Sustainer, and all-loving heavenly Father.

GUIDED PRAYER

1. Meditate on the goodness of God being your perfect Father. What does it mean for your relationship with him if you would truly see him this way? How are you to reorient your perspectives in light of his word?

"For God so loved the world, that he gave his only Son, that whoever believes in him should not perish but have eternal life." John 3:16

"And call no man your father on earth, for you have one Father, who is in heaven." Matthew 23:9

"Every good gift and every perfect gift is from above, coming down from the Father of lights with whom there is no variation or shadow due to change." James 1:17

2. In what ways have you viewed God other than a loving Father? In what ways have you seen him as a taskmaster, distant Creator, or angry or passive Father?

"Is your own personal prayer life characterized by the simplicity, childlike candor, boundless trust, and easy familiarity of a little one crawling up in Daddy's lap? An assured knowing that the daddy doesn't care if the child falls asleep, starts playing with toys, or even starts chatting with little friends, because the daddy knows the child has essentially chosen to be with him for that moment? Is that the spirit of your interior prayer life?" Brennan Manning, *The Furious Longing of God*.

3. Ask God to help you encounter the depths of his love today. Take time to receive his presence and rest in his goodness. Open up any parts of your life that aren't bearing the fruit of his unconditional love and receive all the affection he has to give.

"Blessed be the God and Father of our Lord Jesus Christ, who has blessed us in Christ with every spiritual blessing in the heavenly places." Ephesians 1:3

You are the child of a good, near, and loving Father. Seeing God as your Father not only impacts your perception of him, but also of yourself. You are loved. You are liked. You are enjoyed. The God who only thinks, feels, and says truth values relationship with you enough to send his only Son to die for you. Never let the world or the enemy shake the foundational love of your heavenly Father. No failure, weakness, or sin could ever change the fact that you are loved, accepted, and valued. May you find peace today where there has been only loneliness, pressure, and disatisfaction.

Extended Reading: John 17

The Fruit of Abiding

DEVOTIONAL

So often out of a right desire to do good and God-honoring works we try and force fruit out of ourselves without taking the time to rest and receive the nutrients we can only get from abiding in our heavenly Father. A branch disconnected from an apple tree can no more produce good fruit than you and I can do good works apart from continual abiding in the love, grace, and presence of God. Without truly centering our lives around meeting with God, we'll never produce the fruit we were created to make. Jesus taught us in John 15:1-5,

*"Whoever abides in me and I in him,
he it is that bears much fruit, for apart
from me you can do nothing."*

JOHN 15:5

I am the true vine, and my Father is the vinedresser. Every branch in me that does not bear fruit he takes away, and every branch that does bear fruit he prunes, that it may bear more fruit. Already you are clean because of the word that I have spoken to you. Abide in me, and I in you. As the branch cannot bear fruit by itself, unless it abides in the vine, neither can you, unless you abide in me. I am the vine; you are the branches. Whoever abides in me and I in him, he it is that bears much fruit, for apart from me you can do nothing.

God's heart is for us to abide in him all day, every day. How incredible is that! You and I can graft ourselves every day into the perfect, good, and powerful vine of our heavenly Father. We can wake up every day, open our hearts to God, and live out of the union afforded us by the powerful sacrifice of Jesus.

Rather than striving to do good works from the moment our feet hit the ground, we must take time to be loved by our heavenly Father. Rather than making our own opportunities to serve God, we must allow him to guide us to the works he's set out for us. Rather than trying to lead others to Jesus by our own efforts, we must simply live openly and honestly with others, thereby revealing God's heart to meet with those who are broken and in need of him. And rather than living as if God has left us to our devices, we must acknowledge our union with the Holy Spirit in every moment, thereby allowing his loving presence to permeate everything we do.

James 2:26 teaches, *"For as the body apart from the spirit is dead, so also faith apart from works is dead."* Connect yourself to the wonderful vine of Jesus today. Center your life around meeting with him. It's only in abiding in God that your faith will produce works that are alive, eternal, and filled with the transformational power of God's Spirit. May you discover the freedom and love available to you in continual communion with your heavenly Father today.

GUIDED PRAYER

1. Meditate on the importance of abiding in the vine. Allow Scripture to stir up your desire to rest in God today.

"Be still, and know that I am God. I will be exalted among the nations, I will be exalted in the earth!" Psalm 46:10

"Whoever abides in me and I in him, he it is that bears much fruit, for apart from me you can do nothing." John 15:5

"That which we have seen and heard we proclaim also to you, so that you too may have fellowship with us; and indeed our fellowship is with the Father and with his Son Jesus Christ." 1 John 1:3

2. Where have you been striving to do good works apart from the abiding presence of your Creator? What parts of your life need to have a greater connection to the love of God?

3. Take time to rest in the presence of God. Abide in him. Don't look to or think about the things set before you today. There will be plenty of time for tasks and relationships. Focus all your attention on the reality of God's nearness and open your heart to receive all the love he has for you in this present moment.

The absolute most powerful and good work we can do every day is pursuing continual communion with God. More than God wants us to strive to serve him, he simply wants us to let him love us. More than he wants any work of our hands, he wants our hearts. His love comes without agenda. There is immense value in the children of God simply living in relationship with the Father. Don't let the works-based systems of this world seep into the grace-based relationship you have with God.

Extended Reading: John 15

Jesus is the Center

DAY 19

DEVOTIONAL

All of eternity centers around the life, death, and resurrection of Jesus. He is the all-important, eternity-changing, and humanity-redeeming Son of the living God. Colossians 1:15 tells us, *"He is the image of the invisible God, the firstborn of all creation."* Hebrews 1:3 says, *"He is the radiance of the glory of God and the exact imprint of his nature, and he upholds the universe by the word of his power. After making purification for sins, he sat down at the right hand of the Majesty on high."* And at the time of his return, Revelation 19:16 says, *"On his robe and on his thigh he has a name written, King of kings and Lord of lords."*

"For to us a child is born, to us a son is given; and the government shall be upon his shoulder, and his name shall be called Wonderful Counselor, Mighty God, Everlasting Father, Prince of Peace."

ISAIAH 9:6

To center our lives around meeting with God is to build our foundation on the unshakable center of all eternity. To build our lives around encounters with Jesus is to place the anchor of our hope in the King of kings and Lord of lords. Only Jesus is faithful to his word. Only Jesus will accomplish that which he has promised us.

1 John 2:17 says, *"And the world is passing away along with its desires, but whoever does the will of God abides forever."* The will of God is to center our lives around his loving presence. God's greatest commandment is that we would simply love him with all we do. To live differently than the world around you by centering your life around encountering Jesus is to chart a new path that leads to the fullness of life.

It may appear foolish to the world to place your hope solely in the person of Jesus, but nothing could be more important. It may look different to cast aside the pursuits of society such as comfort, status, and acclaim, but no greater decision could be made. You serve a God who was, is, and is to come. You belong to a King who laid down his life that you might truly live. You'll find no greater joy, peace, or purpose than in serving Jesus alone. There is no greater life than one lived in full devotion to the King of all the earth.

Take time today to recommit yourself fully to the King of kings and Lord of lords. Step away from the limited perspective and think about the divine, eternal kingdom of God. Allow the truth of God's word and love to fill you with the courage to choose devotion to him over service to yourself and the world around you. May your day today be filled with the abiding presence of King Jesus.

GUIDED PRAYER

1. Meditate on Scripture about the person of Jesus. Remember that Jesus is alive and near. He is the living God, and Scripture says your life is wrapped up in him.

"I have been crucified with Christ. It is no longer I who live, but Christ who lives in me. And the life I now live in the flesh I live by faith in the Son of God, who loved me and gave himself for me." Galatians 2:20

"For to us a child is born, to us a son is given; and the government shall be upon his shoulder, and his name shall be called Wonderful Counselor, Mighty God, Everlasting Father, Prince of Peace." Isaiah 9:6

"Looking to Jesus, the founder and perfecter of our faith, who for the joy that was set before him endured the cross, despising the shame, and is seated at the right hand of the throne of God." Hebrews 12:2

2. In what ways is your life not centered around Jesus? In what ways are you living for the earth rather than for eternity?

3. Ask the Holy Spirit to help you center your life around who Jesus was and is. Ask him to fill you with the knowledge of his nearness and love for you. Open your heart and receive the presence of Jesus. Ask him to show you ways that you can center your life around him today.

"If then you have been raised with Christ, seek the things that are above, where Christ is, seated at the right hand of God." Colossians 3:1

Napoleon Bonaparte is quoted as having said, "Alexander, Caesar, Charlemagne, and myself founded empires; but what foundation did we rest the creations of our genius? Upon force. Jesus Christ founded an empire upon love; and at this hour millions of men would die for Him." Is your life so wrapped up in Jesus that you would love and serve him at any cost? If not, know that there is grace. We only come to a place of full devotion by spending time consistently being loved by a selfless, servant-hearted God. May you rest in the grace of your heavenly Father today as you pursue a life centered around your loving Savior.

Extended Reading: Colossians 3

Making the Most of Our Time

DEVOTIONAL

Ephesians 5:15-16 warns us, *"Look carefully then how you walk, not as unwise but as wise, making the best use of the time, because the days are evil."* Our time is of the utmost importance here on earth. We'll never get back the days we spend frivolously pursuing the things of the world. We'll never get back the time spent outside of God's purposes

*"Look carefully then how you walk, not as
unwise but as wise, making the best use of
the time, because the days are evil."*

EPHESIANS 5:15-16

of receiving and giving love. Our time here is too limited and too important to spend on burdens, stresses, sin, and worldly pursuits. If we're going to make the most of this life, we must learn to center our time around the eternal value of meeting with God. It's for this reason James 4:13-15 says,

Come now, you who say, "Today or tomorrow we will go into such and such a town and spend a year there and trade and make a profit"—yet you do not know what tomorrow will bring. What is your life? For you are a mist that appears for a little time and then vanishes. Instead you ought to say, "If the Lord wills, we will live and do this or that."

Looking at the ways in which we spend our time is one of the best ways to assess the posture of our heart. If we spend all our time working for and thinking about the things of the world, we can know that we have not yet come into a right revelation of God's purposes for us. If we spend the majority of our time simply getting through our days trying to find happiness rather than seeking the face of our

heavenly Father that we might receive sustaining, transcendent joy, we can know that we have yet to surrender our lives fully to our King.

The great thing about the nature of time is that it is completely ours to do with what we will. We can, right now, decide to make the best use of our time according to the purposes of God as revealed to us through Scripture. We can, right now, decide to stop wasting precious minutes on that which is fleeting and temporal and instead invest our days in the lasting, eternal, and fruitful purposes of our heavenly Father.

Psalm 90:12 says, *"Teach us to number our days that we may get a heart of wisdom."* God longs to teach us how to use our days wisely. He longs to give us a heart of wisdom that we might center our lives around meeting with him. You have God himself dwelling within you, ready to guide you into a lifestyle of purposeful living. Choose today to open your heart and mind to the Teacher, the very Spirit of God, and live according to his will. May you find peace, joy, and purpose in the ways in which you invest your time today.

GUIDED PRAYER

1. Meditate on the importance of using your time wisely.

"Look carefully then how you walk, not as unwise but as wise, making the best use of the time, because the days are evil." Ephesians 5:15-16

"So teach us to number our days that we may get a heart of wisdom." Psalm 90:12

2. Ask the Holy Spirit to show you any ways in which you've been using your time unwisely.

Know that he is not a God who takes away all the things you enjoy. He's not anti-entertainment, friends, and parties. He's a fun God who truly loves you. Don't mix religion and the heart of your heavenly Father. Trust that whatever he leads you to change will result in the absolute most fun, fruitful, and satisfying way you can live.

"Come now, you who say, 'Today or tomorrow we will go into such and such a town and spend a year there and trade and make a profit'—yet you do not know what tomorrow will bring. What is your life? For you are a mist that appears for a little time and then vanishes. Instead you ought to say, 'If the Lord wills, we will live and do this or that.'" James 4:13-15

3. Ask God to help you spend your time wisely today.
Ask him to help you follow his direction as you go about the day set before you.

"Nevertheless, I tell you the truth: it is to your advantage that I go away, for if I do not go away, the Helper will not come to you. But if I go, I will send him to you." John 16:7

You can trust that God has the absolute best plan for your time. Matthew 6:8 promises, *"Your Father knows what you need before you ask him."* He has every one of your needs sorted out. He will provide for you perfectly. You can trust him with your life and know that your job, family, and circumstances will be better in the capable and loving hands of your heavenly Father. Devote your time, job, money, and relationships to him that they might be filled with the blessing of God.

Extended Reading: Ephesians 5

Living from Union

DEVOTIONAL

One of the greatest scandals of the Christian faith is that God himself, in all his holiness and love, would dwell in the heart of man. You and I have been brought into union with God by the blood of Jesus. Nothing can separate us from him any longer. He is closer than our breath. He is more real than the very ground beneath our feet.

The New Testament is filled with truth about our union with God. Galatians 2:20 says, *"I have been crucified with Christ. It is no longer I who live, but Christ who lives*

> *"I have been crucified with Christ. It is no longer I who live, but Christ who lives in me. And the life I now live in the flesh I live by faith in the Son of God, who loved me and gave himself for me."*
>
> GALATIANS 2:20

in me. And the life I now live in the flesh I live by faith in the Son of God, who loved me and gave himself for me." 1 Corinthians 6:19-20 says, *"Or do you not know that your body is a temple of the Holy Spirit within you, whom you have from God? You are not your own, for you were bought with a price. So glorify God in your body."* Romans 6:4 says, *"We were buried therefore with him by baptism into death, in order that, just as Christ was raised from the dead by the glory of the Father, we too might walk in newness of life."* And Colossians 1:27 says, *"To them God chose to make known how great among the Gentiles are the riches of the glory of this mystery, which is Christ in you, the hope of glory."*

There is never a single moment that you are apart from God. God is in you and with you through every trial, success, victory, and defeat. He is for you and available to you all day, every day. Even in our sin, God remains. Even in our rebellion, God dwells within us. What's left for us to do is learn how to allow this union to permeate every area of our lives. To work out our salvation is to learn to cast aside that which belongs to our former self and live out of our new identity as unified with Christ himself.

If we're going to truly center our lives around meeting with God, we must learn to acknowledge the fact that he is already with us. He is not a distant God who has to travel from his throne in heaven down to us whenever we make time for him. He's not a God who only dwells in churches, fellowships, ministries, or clergy. He is the God who dwells within you, loves you, likes you, and longs to be with you in constant communion.

Take time today to renew your mind to the truth of your union with God. Ask him to reveal his nearness that you might *"walk in newness of life"* today (Romans 6:4). Make space in your heart and mind to allow the presence of God to permeate every area of your life. May today mark a radical change in your life as God himself begins to move, work, bless, and speak in all you do.

GUIDED PRAYER

1. Meditate on your union with God. Renew your mind by placing your trust in Scripture rather than your feelings or past experiences.

"I have been crucified with Christ. It is no longer I who live, but Christ who lives in me. And the life I now live in the flesh I live by faith in the Son of God, who loved me and gave himself for me." Galatians 2:20

"Therefore, if anyone is in Christ, he is a new creation. The old has passed away; behold, the new has come." 2 Corinthians 5:17

"Or do you not know that your body is a temple of the Holy Spirit within you, whom you have from God? You are not your own." 1 Corinthians 6:19-20

2. What areas of your life are not marked by union with the Holy Spirit? Where are you doing life as if God isn't with you? Where are you striving and working for that which is already yours in Christ Jesus?

3. Ask the Holy Spirit to reveal his nearness. Ask him to help you be a person who receives rather than strives and who rests rather than toils.

"Be still, and know that I am God." Psalm 46:10

Oftentimes we take feelings of loneliness, rejection, shame, and guilt and believe that they must be truth. Truth isn't found in our emotions, but rather in the word of God. Our mind is the gateway to our emotions. We feel the way we do because of what we perceive and believe. If we engage in the process of renewing our mind to God's word, our emotions will get in line with truth. You and God are one. There is nothing you or anyone else can do to change that. May the truth of Scripture guide you into a lifestyle of centering your life around the union already available to you in Christ.

Extended Reading: 2 Corinthians 5

God longs to be encountered

04

WEEK

"Draw near to God, and he will draw near to you." James 4:8

WEEKLY OVERVIEW

One of the most scandalous truths of the gospel is that our Creator longs to be encountered by his creation. God longs to meet with us. His greatest desire is for relationship with us. I can't fathom why God in all his holiness and goodness makes himself available to us, but it is the powerful truth of Scripture. God is pursuing each of us with his relentless love, seeking out those who might respond to his open invitation by opening the door of their hearts to him. My prayer is that in response to God's desire to meet with his people we would be those who say yes to centering our lives around his nearness. May your week be marked by the reality of God's presence and love.

God Longs to be Encountered

DAY 22

DEVOTIONAL

We serve a God who longs to be encountered. Our God is not distant. He is not a recluse. Every morning there is an open invitation set before us to encounter the peaceful, tangible presence of the living God. In fact, it's because of God's desire to be encountered that Scripture so often commands us to seek him. He is not a God who hides, but he is also not a God who forces himself on us. He quietly beckons us to a life marked by his nearness, asking us to seek him that our heart might be open and receptive to him.

"The Lord looks down from heaven on the children of man, to see if there are any who understand, who seek after God."

PSALM 14:2

1 Chronicles 16:11 commands us, *"Seek the Lord and his strength; seek his presence continually!"* And Revelation 3:20 says, *"Behold, I stand at the door and knock. If anyone hears my voice and opens the door, I will come in to him and eat with him, and he with me."* May we be a people who center our lives around God's longing to be encountered. May we seek him with all we are.

I've lived so much of my life as if I'm on my own. I was without a true revelation of just how close God is to me. I was without a true knowledge that the God I serve longs to be known by me. You see, the foundation for my spending time with God was that I should, not that he actually desired relationship with me. As soon as I got a glimpse into the heart of my heavenly Father to simply love me and enjoy me, I was hooked.

No matter who you are or what you've done, you serve a God who longs to meet with you. He is knocking on the door of your heart today, asking you to simply let him come in. He is quietly beckoning you with his love, simply speaking to you, "Don't shut me out." God has an incredible life filled with an ever-increasing awareness of his love for you. He longs for your heart to be wrapped up in his presence when the world rejects you, speaks lies to you, or tries to pull you away from the comfort of his love and peace.

Hebrews 11:6 says, *"And without faith it is impossible to please him, for whoever would draw near to God must believe that he exists and that he rewards those who seek him."* Seek the presence of your heavenly Father today in faith that he longs to be encountered. Trust him at his word that he will reward your seeking with the wonders of his nearness. Seek a deeper, more intimate relationship with him in light of the truth that he is always fully available to you. May your life be ever filled with communion with your loving heavenly Father.

GUIDED PRAYER

1. Meditate on God's desire to be encountered. Allow Scripture to stir up your faith to meet with God.

"Behold, I stand at the door and knock. If anyone hears my voice and opens the door, I will come in to him and eat with him, and he with me." Revelation 3:20

"Ask, and it will be given to you; seek, and you will find; knock, and it will be opened to you. For everyone who asks receives, and the one who seeks finds, and to the one who knocks it will be opened." Matthew 7:7-8

"And you, Solomon my son, know the God of your father and serve him with a whole heart and with a willing mind, for the Lord searches all hearts and understands every plan and thought. If you seek him, he will be found by you, but if you forsake him, he will cast you off forever." 1 Chronicles 28:9

2. What have you believed about encountering God that doesn't line up with his heart and his word? Where do you feel like you can't encounter God? What parts of your life are absent of his presence and the fruit of his nearness?

3. Seek the presence of God today. Take time to open your heart and in faith trust that you can encounter God. Commit yourself to centering your day around his presence and doing nothing apart from an awareness of his nearness.

"The Lord is good to those who wait for him, to the soul who seeks him." Lamentations 3:25

"The Lord looks down from heaven on the children of man, to see if there are any who understand, who seek after God." Psalm 14:2

"Draw near to God, and he will draw near to you." James 4:8

How amazing is the heart of our heavenly Father that he longs to be encountered! Through the powerful sacrifice of Jesus we can live in communion with God. Jesus paid the highest price for us to simply have close relationship with our Creator. Let us not be a people who forsake the sacrifice of Jesus. If God would send his only Son to die that we might live in relationship with him, it must be absolutely the best thing in this life. Taste and see how good your God is today. Let him into all you do. May your life be filled with the presence of God as you open the door of your heart to the reality of his nearness.

Extended Reading: Revelation 3:14-4:11

God Longs for Us to Know His Love

DAY 23

DEVOTIONAL

I've spent so much of my life striving to be loved. The overwhelming need to be loved by somebody, anybody, is at the heart of most every decision, thought, perspective, and action I make. We are created with a longing to be loved. God formed us with an insatiable need for love because he desires to satisfy that longing. You see, we no longer have to go through life wondering if we're loved. Our God doesn't hide his heart from us. He never holds back his love.

Romans 5:8 says, *"But God shows his love for us in that while we were still sinners, Christ died for us."* God

demonstrated his love for us on the cross. But the cross also serves as a reminder that God will, now and forever, continually pour out his love. Not only did he commit a powerful act of love then, but he also makes his love available to us now.

Psalm 26:3 says, *"For your steadfast love is before my eyes, and I walk in your faithfulness."* And Psalm 36:5 says, *"Your steadfast love, O Lord, extends to the heavens, your faithfulness to the clouds."* The love of God is continually available to us. His steadfast love is here, ready to be experienced. God longs to so

> *"No, in all these things we are more than conquerors through him who loved us. For I am sure that neither death nor life, nor angels nor rulers, nor things present nor things to come, nor powers, nor height nor depth, nor anything else in all creation, will be able to separate us from the love of God in Christ Jesus our Lord."*

ROMANS 8:37-39

satisfy our great need for love that we stop seeking it from the world. He longs to so fill us up with his unconditional affections that we would no longer strive to be loved, but simply find rest in him.

Romans 8:37-39 says,
No, in all these things we are more than conquerors through him who loved us. For I am sure that neither death nor life, nor angels nor rulers, nor things present nor things to come, nor powers, nor height nor depth, nor anything else in all creation, will be able to separate us from the love of God in Christ Jesus our Lord.

There is nothing we could ever do to separate ourselves from the love of God. As soon as we feel the need to be loved we can always turn our hearts toward our heavenly Father and simply receive a fresh awareness of his powerful, unconditional love. Stop working to be loved. Stop striving for that which is already yours. What are the affections of man in comparison to the love of your Creator? What is the fleeting, fickle praise of man in comparison to the all-consuming, powerful, and truthful love of God? May your life be marked by a peace that comes from resting in the love of your heavenly Father alone.

GUIDED PRAYER

1. Reflect on your need for love. In what ways do you strive to be loved every day? Who have you been seeking out love from to fill a need in your life? Where have you been striving for the opinion of man?

2. Meditate on the unconditional nature of God's love. Meditate on the availability of his presence.

"But God shows his love for us in that while we were still sinners, Christ died for us." Romans 5:8

"For God so loved the world, that he gave his only Son, that whoever believes in him should not perish but have eternal life." John 3:16

"No, in all these things we are more than conquerors through him who loved us. For I am sure that neither death nor life, nor angels nor rulers, nor things present nor things to come, nor powers, nor height nor depth, nor anything else in all creation, will be able to separate us from the love of God in Christ Jesus our Lord." Romans 8:37-39

3. Ask the Holy Spirit to help you encounter to love of God today. Ask God how he feels about you and wait for a sense of his love. Rest in the truth of Scripture and receive the love of your heavenly Father.

"For your steadfast love is before my eyes, and I walk in your faithfulness." Psalm 26:3

"Your steadfast love, O Lord, extends to the heavens, your faithfulness to the clouds." Psalm 36:5

One of the most powerful truths about God's love can be found in 1 John 4:18. Scripture says, *"There is no fear in love, but perfect love casts out fear. For fear has to do with punishment, and whoever fears has not been perfected in love."* God's love makes us fearless. Who or what is there to fear when the God of the universe truly loves us? What cause is there for fear when God would send his only Son to die that we might simply have relationship with him? Rest in the love of God today and allow the truth of his affections for you to cast out any fear you have. There is no reason to fear. God has you and loves you. May you find peace and joy today in response to the steadfast love of your heavenly Father.

Extended Reading: 1 John 4

God Longs for Us to Know His Voice

DAY 24

DEVOTIONAL

I've spent so much of my life as a believer thinking that God was silent, or at least only spoke through the Bible, others, and situations. While God most definitely does speak in those ways, he also longs to speak directly to his children. Scripture is laden with story after story of God's people hearing his voice and responding in obedience. From the Old Testament to the New Testament, God clearly speaks to his people. The question before us today is, will we make space to listen?

"Call to me and I will answer you, and
will tell you great and hidden things
that you have not known."

JEREMIAH 33:3

John 8:47 says, *"Whoever is of God hears the words of God."* And John 10:27 says, *"My sheep hear my voice, and I know them, and they follow me."* We serve a God who desires his voice to be known. God is not silent. He is not quiet. Our heavenly Father longs to guide us, tell us his heart for us, and do life with us. He's longing for a relationship with you filled with continual conversation.

Hearing God's voice is not only for a select few. It isn't only for the Christian elite or those who spend all day, every day meditating and praying. We as believers hear God's voice first and foremost because he wants to speak to us. We can hear God's voice by grace alone.

So what does it sound like to hear God's voice? Through the Holy Spirit God is able to speak in clearer and more profound ways than a conversation between you and me. 1 Corinthians 3:16 says, *"Do you not know that you are God's temple and that God's Spirit dwells in you?"* The Holy Spirit is with you right now. And because he dwells within us he has the ability to speak to our heart. He can speak with words or give an intuition or knowledge about something. He can fill us with peace about a decision and give us a feeling of unrest when we're doing something that isn't his will. God can speak to us in ways more intimate and clear than any other conversation because there is nothing in the way of us and him.

But God will never force his voice on us. He is not a God who yells into the chaos and attempts to drown out all the other voices. He is a God of peace and patience who waits for us to open our heart to him and listen. Take time today to open your heart and acknowledge the voice of your Father. Make space in all the busyness to simply listen to whatever he would say. Ask him any questions you have of him and trust that he will speak perfectly whatever it is he wants to say to you.

May your day be filled with continual conversation with your loving, present heavenly Father.

123

GUIDED PRAYER

1. Meditate on the availability of hearing God speak. Reflect on all the ways he speaks and allow Scripture to fill your heart with faith to have a conversation with your heavenly Father.

"And your ears shall hear a word behind you, saying, 'This is the way, walk in it,' when you turn to the right or when you turn to the left." Isaiah 30:21

"When the Spirit of truth comes, he will guide you into all the truth, for he will not speak on his own authority, but whatever he hears he will speak, and he will declare to you the things that are to come." John 16:13

"My sheep hear my voice, and I know them, and they follow me." John 10:27

2. Take time to quiet your soul and receive God's presence. Ask him to reveal his nearness to you. Have faith that the Holy Spirit is with you right now.

"Do you not know that you are God's temple and that God's Spirit dwells in you?" 1 Corinthians 3:16

3. Ask God to tell you how he feels about you in this moment. Ask him to speak to you anything he wants you to know. Have patience and pay attention to any changes in your feelings or anything you hear in your spirit.

"Call to me and I will answer you, and will tell you great and hidden things that you have not known." Jeremiah 33:3

"O Lord, in the morning you hear my voice; in the morning I prepare a sacrifice for you and watch." Psalm 5:3

"Blessed rather are those who hear the word of God and keep it!" Luke 11:28

While hearing the voice of God can sound a little "out there," it is wholly biblical. Our God is alive and active. He is not distant, and he longs for us to truly know him. Allow Scripture to define your reality rather than past experiences or worldly perceptions. The spiritual is wholly real. God's presence is real. The fact that he dwells within us, speaks, guides, gives revelation, heals, and saves is the reality all of us live in whether we acknowledge it or not. Open your heart to God today and allow him to guide you into a lifestyle of greater communion with him. Live today in the fullness of relationship available to you in the Holy Spirit. May you hear the loving, close voice of the Holy Spirit throughout your day today as you open your heart to him.

Extended Reading: John 10

God Longs for Us to Know His Truth

DEVOTIONAL

In the incredible, abundant blessings of Scripture and the Holy Spirit, God has demonstrated his longing for us to know truth. Truth is a powerful weapon against the schemes of the enemy. Truth has an ability to bestow confidence and freedom on all who find their satisfaction in it. And truth in the eyes of God is completely founded in relationship with the person of Jesus Christ. May God grant us a hunger for truth that is deeply satisfied in communion with our loving Savior today.

Everything God is and does is truth personified. There is no lie or deceit in our God. And therefore it is only in centering our lives around relationship with him that we will begin to experience the fruit of truth in our lives. In John 14:6 Jesus says, *"I am the way, and the truth, and the life. No one comes to the Father except through me."* The life of Jesus is our example of truth. Everything he did was a perfect demonstration of truth. If we don't devote ourselves to the study of his life and experiencing who he is personally, we'll find ourselves living on the rocky shores of indecision and half-truths. We need his example to follow.

We need the life of Jesus at the forefront of our minds if we are to enjoy the abundant life that truth has to offer us. 1 John 5:20 says, *"And we know that the Son of God has come and has given us understanding, so that we may know him who is true; and we are in him who is true, in his Son Jesus Christ. He is the true*

*"And you will know the truth, and
the truth will set you free."*

JOHN 8:32

God and eternal life." Jesus is the Word made flesh. And through the Holy Spirit and Scripture, we have access to not only learning about his life, but being transformed into his likeness.

Romans 8:29 says, *"For those whom he foreknew he also predestined to be conformed to the image of his Son, in order that he might be the firstborn among many brothers."* You and I are created to seek truth and see it come to fruition in our lives. We are created to shine the powerful light of truth into a world filled with the darkness of lies and deceit. But before we can share the truth of God, we must allow it to fill and transform us. 1 John 3:18 says, *"Little children, let us not love in word or talk but in deed and in truth."* Truth is meant to manifest itself in our actions. Truth is so much more about our deeds of love than the words we say. Anyone can say words and not truly mean it. No one can truly love someone without revealing to them Jesus, truth made manifest in flesh. We can't love someone without the power of truth shining forth into the core of who we are, that God loves us unconditionally just as we are.

Take time today to allow the truth of God's love and Jesus' life to make its way into every part of your life. Continue the process of being conformed to the image of Jesus by meditating on Scripture and experiencing the living, active person of Jesus today. May the truth of God's love lead you to a life of enjoying God's presence and loving others well.

GUIDED PRAYER

1. Meditate on the importance of knowing and experiencing truth. Allow Scripture to stir up your desires to seek truth.

"And you will know the truth, and the truth will set you free." John 8:32

"The Lord is near to all who call on him, to all who call on him in truth." Psalm 145:18

"Of his own will he brought us forth by the word of truth, that we should be a kind of firstfruits of his creatures." James 1:18

2. Where is the truth of God not shining forth out of you in deed? Where are you not experiencing the fruit of truth in your life?

"Little children, let us not love in word or talk but in deed and in truth." 1 John 3:18

3. Give that area of your life to God and ask him to transform you into the likeness of Jesus today.

Meditate on truth centered around that area and allow it to sink down from your head to your heart. Make space to let God fully love you and ask the Holy Spirit to help you love others well throughout your day.

"When the Spirit of truth comes, he will guide you into all the truth, for he will not speak on his own authority, but whatever he hears he will speak, and he will declare to you the things that are to come." John 16:13

God longs to reveal himself to you and fully love you today. He longs for you to taste and see his goodness. To grow in godly truth isn't like taking a class or learning a subject; it's all about relationship. May the truth of Scripture be revealed to you in relationship with the living, active God. May you experience firsthand the God of the Bible and see truth in the man of Jesus. And may your life be a better reflection of God's love today as his truth works its way into every part of your life.

Extended Reading: 1 John 5

God Longs to Share His Will

DAY 26

DEVOTIONAL

One of the most peaceful truths of Scripture is that God longs to share his will with his people. God is not one who leaves us to our own devices. He's not even one who leaves us with the Bible and says, "Good luck. I hope you figure it out." He's the God who dwells within us, longing to speak into our lives and guide us into his perfect, pleasing plans.

"And the Lord will guide you continually and satisfy your desire in scorched places and make your bones strong; and you shall be like a watered garden, like a spring of water, whose waters do not fail."

ISAIAH 58:11

Jeremiah 29:11-14 is an often quoted passage in Christian circles. But I pray that the powerful promise contained in its words will be revealed to you today in a fresh, transformative way. Scripture says,

For I know the plans I have for you, declares the Lord, plans for welfare and not for evil, to give you a future and a hope. Then you will call upon me and come and pray to me, and I will hear you. You will seek me and find me, when you seek me with all your heart. I will be found by you, declares the Lord, and I will restore your fortunes and gather you from all the nations and all the places where I have driven you, declares the Lord, and I will bring you back to the place from which I sent you into exile.

We can place our hope in the revealed will of our heavenly Father. We can trust that we are not sheep without a shepherd, but rather those in the flock of a perfect, loving God who came to lay down his life for us. Through the Holy Spirit, God is perfectly capable of guiding us into his plans for *"welfare and not for evil."* Behind his leading is always a more abundant, presence-filled life. Behind his leading is always more of him and more of who we are in him.

Proverbs 3:5-6 says, *"Trust in the Lord with all your heart, and do not lean on your own understanding. In all your ways acknowledge him, and he will make straight your paths."* God longs to make straight our paths. But in order to follow his leading, we must assess where our trust is and who we are acknowledging with our lives. We will never follow that which we don't fully trust. If we are to be led by the Spirit we must trust that everything he tells us to do is absolutely the best thing for us.

Trust is meant to be the fruit of relationship. It's meant to be birthed out of an experiential knowledge of God's trustworthiness. If you haven't given God much of a chance to prove himself trustworthy in your life, today is the day. We as the people of God must place our hope in him alone if we are to experience all the wealth of life his promises have to offer. We must place our trust in him if we are to receive a full knowledge of his will.

Take time to meditate on the trustworthiness of your God. Meditate on his desire to share with you his will. Take time to place your trust in him alone and commit yourself to following his leading. May your day be marked by all the fruit of God's perfect, pleasing plans for your life.

131

GUIDED PRAYER

1. Meditate on God's trustworthiness and desire to share his will with you.

"And the Lord will guide you continually and satisfy your desire in scorched places and make your bones strong; and you shall be like a watered garden, like a spring of water, whose waters do not fail." Isaiah 58:11

"For I know the plans I have for you, declares the Lord, plans for welfare and not for evil, to give you a future and a hope. Then you will call upon me and come and pray to me, and I will hear you. You will seek me and find me, when you seek me with all your heart. I will be found by you, declares the Lord, and I will restore your fortunes and gather you from all the nations and all the places where I have driven you, declares the Lord, and I will bring you back to the place from which I sent you into exile." Jeremiah 29:11-14

2. Where do you have a hard time trusting God? Where is your life not marked by his perfect, pleasing plans?

"The heart of man plans his way, but the Lord establishes his steps." Proverbs 16:9

3. Ask God to reveal his will to you in those areas. Align your heart with his desires for you that you might experience the fruit of truly following his will. Place your trust in God alone for every area of your life.

"Trust in the Lord with all your heart, and do not lean on your own understanding. In all your ways acknowledge him, and he will make straight your paths." Proverbs 3:5-6

"Do not be conformed to this world, but be transformed by the renewal of your mind, that by testing you may discern what is the will of God, what is good and acceptable and perfect." Romans 12:2

Oftentimes God's perfect, pleasing plans don't conform to the desires and wants of the world. But we have to place our trust in him that his ways are higher than ours. His desires and wants for us are better than anything we can imagine. He has eternity in mind when he leads us along with our present circumstances and desires. Trust that as you align your heart with him and place your hope in him alone, his leading will perfectly satisfy the deep desires of your heart.

Extended Reading: Isaiah 58

Mystery is to be Sought Out

DAY 27

DEVOTIONAL

The fact that God conceals things in mystery for his children to search out is one of the most curious and wonderful truths of Scripture. Proverbs 25:2 says, *"It is the glory of God to conceal things, but the glory of kings is to search things out."* We who have been made kings and queens by the blood of Jesus have been granted access to the mysteries of God. God in his grace has given us the right to know the mind of Christ (1 Corinthians 2:16).

"It is the glory of God to conceal things, but the glory of kings is to search things out."

PROVERBS 25:2

What would relationship with the God of the universe be without mystery? What would it be like to know the God who has formed galaxies and planets beyond anything we will ever discover without that which remains unknown? We are made to be enthralled by the mysteries of our heavenly Father. We are created to search out that which is not made plain to us. God is inviting us to ask, question, seek, and find that which transcends the natural and stretches into the unknown: the eternal.

Colossians 2:1–3 says,

For I want you to know how great a struggle I have for you and for those at Laodicea and for all who have not seen me face to face, that their hearts may be encouraged, being knit together in love, to reach all the riches of full assurance of understanding and the knowledge of God's mystery, which is Christ, in whom are hidden all the treasures of wisdom and knowledge.

All mystery finds its resolve in the person of Jesus Christ. Within him dwells *"all the treasures of wisdom and knowledge."* And the more we get to know the living, active person of Jesus through his Spirit, the more we receive important, transformative revelation. You see, even something as foundational to the Christian faith as grace is laden with mystery. The powerful effects of Jesus' grace-filled sacrifice baffle the mind. How could one man in laying down his life make righteousness and salvation available to all? But in God's grace this is wholly possible. And only when we truly seek out the mysteries laden within grace will we begin to experience all the powerful effects it has to offer us.

May we as God's children grow to love the mysteries laid open for us by our loving heavenly Father. May we enjoy the process of searching out the deeper things within God's heart with the help of the Holy Spirit. And may that which is unseen, heavenly, and eternal begin to have a profound impact on our perspectives, emotions, thoughts, and actions. Search out the mysteries of your faith today and discover just how vast and available the love of your heavenly Father is for you.

GUIDED PRAYER

1. Meditate on the call before you to search out the deeper things of God. Allow Scripture to stir up your desire for the mysteries of your faith.

"It is the glory of God to conceal things, but the glory of kings is to search things out." Proverbs 25:2

"In my flesh I am filling up what is lacking in Christ's afflictions for the sake of his body, that is, the church, of which I became a minister according to the stewardship from God that was given to me for you, to make the word of God fully known, the mystery hidden for ages and generations but now revealed to his saints. To them God *chose to make known how great among the Gentiles are the riches of the glory of this mystery, which is Christ in you, the hope of glory."* Colossians 1:24-27

2. What parts of your faith have you yet to fully search out? Ask God to reveal what mysteries he's laying open before you that you might walk in a deeper revelation of who he is and what he's done.

3. Take time to search out an aspect of your relationship with God. It might be something about his creation or an aspect like grace, forgiveness, or love.

"You have said, 'Seek my face.' My heart says to you, 'Your face, Lord, do I seek.'" Psalm 27:8

"For I want you to know how great a struggle I have for you and for those at Laodicea and for all who have not seen me face to face, that their hearts may be encouraged, being knit together in love, to reach all the riches of full assurance of understanding and the knowledge of God's mystery, which is Christ, in whom are hidden all the treasures of wisdom and knowledge." Colossians 2:1-3

Coupled with God's desire for us to seek out mystery is the truth that we are not meant to fully grasp every part of God and Christianity. Part of the beauty of our relationship with an omnipotent, omnipresent, and eternal God is that there will always be parts of him that are a mystery to us. How God has always existed and is both three and one are paradoxes too great for comprehension. We must simply trust the truth of Scripture for what it is at times and not dwell on that which we cannot attain. We must reconcile only that which is intended to be reconciled. May you search out all the mysteries opened to you by the blood of Jesus and the Holy Spirit who dwells within you, while at the same time enjoying all the unknowables meant to stir up awe and wonder within you.

Extended Reading: Colossians 1

Do We Know Him?

DAY 28

DEVOTIONAL

Of all that God longs to reveal to us, his children, he most desires that we would simply come to know him. Of all the great mysteries, truths, plans, and longings of his heart, he most desires that we would find all our satisfaction, joy, and purpose in relationship. Jeremiah 9:23-24 describes this profound desire in the heart of God. Scripture says,

> *"Let not the wise man boast in his wisdom, let not the mighty man boast in his might, let not the rich man boast in his riches, but let him who boasts boast in this, that he understands and knows me, that I am the Lord who practices steadfast love, justice, and righteousness in the earth. For in these things I delight, declares the Lord."*

JEREMIAH 9:23-24

Let not the wise man boast in his wisdom, let not the mighty man boast in his might, let not the rich man boast in his riches, but let him who boasts boast in this, that he understands and knows me, that I am the Lord who practices steadfast love, justice, and righteousness in the earth. For in these things I delight, declares the Lord.

What greater knowledge is there than that of God? What greater pursuit exists than knowing the heart of our Creator, the God who would lay down his life to make himself available to us? You and I can know God in deeper, more transformative ways than we can know anyone else. Through the blood of Christ, God has made himself more available and nearer to us than we have yet to discover.

Psalm 46:10 is a powerful and incredible command of the Lord. Our heavenly Father says to us, *"Be still, and know that I am God."* In a world wrought with the hectic chaos of task after task, God says to us, "Be still and simply know me." In a world founded on the principles of earn and receive, God has an open invitation before us to know him apart from any merit of our own. We can know God simply because he desires to be known. We can know God simply because he loves us right now, as we are.

More than God desires any work of our hands or any gifting he could place within us, he wants us to know him. So often we get caught up in the works of the kingdom and forget that our chief purpose in life is simply to be enjoyed by God and to enjoy him in return. This life is meant to be about relationship above all else. It's meant to be about continually encountering the heart of our heavenly Father that we so often live without.

Out of all that we know, may we know God himself the best. Out of all the knowledge and wisdom we can gain from Scripture, may our highest pursuit be a true, intimate knowledge of its Author. Out of all the earth-shattering works set before us, may we know the God whom we serve. And at the end of our days, may our lives have been chiefly marked by a true, passionate, intimate relationship with our heavenly Father.

GUIDED PRAYER

1. Meditate on the availability of knowing God. Allow Scripture to stir up your desire to know God above all else.

"And this is eternal life, that they know you the only true God, and Jesus Christ whom you have sent." John 17:3

"Be still, and know that I am God." Psalm 46:10

2. What pursuits are higher in your life than knowing your heavenly Father? What is a higher priority to you than simply having relationship with God? Take an honest look at your heart, time, actions, and perspectives.

3. Ask the Lord to help you be someone who is simply enjoyed by him and enjoys him. Ask him to help you cast aside all other pursuits that aren't in line with this chief pursuit. Make space and time to *"Be still, and know that [he] is God"* Psalm 46:10.

"But grow in the grace and knowledge of our Lord and Savior Jesus Christ. To him be the glory both now and to the day of eternity. Amen." 2 Peter 3:18

"Let not the wise man boast in his wisdom, let not the mighty man boast in his might, let not the rich man boast in his riches, but let him who boasts boast in this, that he understands and knows me, that I am the Lord who practices steadfast love, justice, and righteousness in the earth. For in these things I delight, declares the Lord." Jeremiah 9:23-24

Recentering our lives around relationship with God is a process in which God has total patience and grace. He knows that you will only center your life around that which you chiefly enjoy. He knows it takes time for him to become your chief joy. But this is most definitely the highest, most important process you can pursue. When he becomes your chief joy, all other aspects of life find their proper place. When he becomes your chief joy, your emotions will no longer be subject to the fickle, fleeting things of the world, but rather grounded in the unshakable, unchanging nature of your heavenly Father. May you offer your whole heart to God today that you might fully enjoy him. May his love and presence be the foundation of your life. And may you seek relationship with him above all else.

Extended Reading: Psalm 46

Abiding in the true vine

"Abide in me, and I in you. As the branch cannot bear fruit by itself, unless it abides in the vine, neither can you, unless you abide in me." John 15:4

The absolute, most important single act of the children of God is making space to encounter our heavenly Father in the secret place. Abiding in God is the foundation on which every other aspect of the Christian life finds success. It establishes roots which enable us to receive all that we need to bear the fruit of the Spirit. It guides us to constant refreshment and revival in God's presence, thereby supplying and sustaining the abundant life God intends for us. My prayer is that you would be marked by wonderful, satisfying, and fulfilling encounters with the presence of God as we look at John 15:1-17 this week. Make room in your heart and mind to rest in the love of your heavenly Father as we look at the different ways we are to abide in true vine of God.

Abide in
the Vine

DAY 29

DEVOTIONAL

I am amazed at the ways in which all of creation visibly demonstrates important spiritual principles. Romans 1:20 says, *"For his invisible attributes, namely, his eternal power and divine nature, have been clearly perceived, ever since the creation of the world, in the things that have been made."* Job 12:7-9 says, *"But ask the beasts, and they will teach you; the birds of the heavens, and they will tell you; or the bushes of the earth, and they will teach you; and the fish of the sea will declare to you. Who among all these does not know that the hand of the Lord has done this?"* All throughout the Gospels, Jesus likens spiritual principles to the surrounding creation. From the parables of the mustard seed (Matthew 13:31-32) and pearl of great price

"Abide in me, and I in you. As the branch cannot bear fruit by itself, unless it abides in the vine, neither can you, unless you abide in me."

JOHN 15:4

(Matthew 13:45-46) to his teaching on the grass of the field and birds of the air (Matthew 6:25-34), clearly God uses creation to illustrate important spiritual principles we need to adopt as believers.

One such important principle is found in John 15:1-17. In verse 4 Jesus says, *"Abide in me, and I in you. As the branch cannot bear fruit by itself, unless it abides in the vine, neither can you, unless you abide in me."* Reflect for a minute on the process of a vine bearing fruit. It takes time, patience, and consistent nourishment for fruit to form on the branches of the vine. So it is with you and me in God. We have the most abundant source of life available to us in God. God waits, patiently beckoning us to simply come and abide in him that we might bear the fruit of abundant life. And once fruit is cut off from the vine it loses its source of life. In order to consistently bear the fruit of God, we have to go back to our vine time and time again to receive all that God longs to give us.

You are created for intimacy with your heavenly Father. Just as God designed grapes to only grow in connection to the vine, you are designed for intimacy with God as your one, true source. There is no other supply of true life. There is no other process by which we experience abundant life outside of abiding in him. Spending time resting in his presence and receiving what he longs to give us is the most important thing you can do on a daily basis. The days we try and bear fruit apart from him are the days we will be overrun with the cares and stresses of this life. The Holy Spirit longs to fill you with the fruit of his presence every moment of every day. All that is required of you is to submit to the reality of his presence rather than go your own way. Choose to listen and receive from him rather than leaning on your own understanding.

By God's grace we can always return to him as our source. It is never too late for us to connect ourselves to the vine and receive the life only God can give. It is never too late to experience the revitalization that can only come through encountering him. And it is never too late for us to bear fruit of eternal value. God has wonderful plans for you that begin today. His mercies are new every morning. The Bible promises in James 4:8, *"Draw near to God, and he will draw near to you."*

Take time to submit yourself to God as your source, receive all that he longs to give you, and find your satisfaction in the reality of his powerful presence.

149

GUIDED PRAYER

1. Meditate on your need to be continually connected to God, your true vine.

"Abide in me, and I in you. As the branch cannot bear fruit by itself, unless it abides in the vine, neither can you, unless you abide in me." John 15:4

2. Ask God to make his presence known to you.
Believe his word that his presence is real and tangible and that you can experience him by his grace.

"And without faith it is impossible to please him, for whoever would draw near to God must believe that he exists and that he rewards those who seek him." Hebrews 11:6

3. Draw near to your God and find life in his presence. Allow his nearness to heal the broken and weary places of your life. Let his Spirit flood the dry areas with his perfect love. Have patience and rest in God. Be slow to speak and move as the Spirit lays a foundation for you to continually bear the fruit of his presence in your life.

"But the fruit of the Spirit is love, joy, peace, patience, kindness, goodness, faithfulness, gentleness, self-control; against such things there is no law." Galatians 5:22-23

As believers we are created to live, think, act, and feel with the Holy Spirit. We were never intended to do life apart from God's presence, and through the life, death and resurrection of Jesus, we don't have to. We've been filled with the very Spirit of God himself who longs to shepherd us into the deeper things of God. May we have the humility to acknowledge our need of God and the faith to believe that he is real and will guide us into a better, more fruitful life in him.

Extended Reading: John 15:1-17

Abiding in the Heartbeat of God

DAY 30

DEVOTIONAL

Jesus makes us an almost unbelievable promise in John 15:7-8. Scripture says, *"If you abide in me, and my words abide in you, ask whatever you wish, and it will be done for you. By this my Father is glorified, that you bear much fruit and so prove to be my disciples."* Jesus promises that if we abide in him and allow his words to abide in us, then we can ask anything we desire of God and it will happen. Clearly this is a vital passage for us to understand today. I believe that the Lord has fresh revelation in store for us if we will take him at his word and allow him to transform our understanding of what it is to petition our heavenly Father. So, let's open our hearts and minds and allow the Holy Spirit to come and do a work in us today as we place our trust in Jesus' word.

"If you abide in me, and my words abide in you, ask whatever you wish, and it will be done for you. By this my Father is glorified, that you bear much fruit and so prove to be my disciples."

JOHN 15:7-8

I have spent a large part of my Christian life praying without understanding how to pray. I used to view prayer as time for me to ask God for what I thought would be good and then wait to see if my circumstances lined up with my prayer. Then only through my circumstances would I know if God's answer to my prayer was yes or no. Then I read John 15:7-8. Jesus clearly teaches a very different model of prayer than I had been experiencing.

Jesus' model for prayer is abiding in his presence, abiding in his words, and then asking God for our heart's desires. God desires that we would be so in tune with his heartbeat and so saturated with his word that our desires would be transformed into his desires. His plan is to fill us with the knowledge of his perfect will for our lives in the secret place so that we can pray and live wholeheartedly with full expectation that our heavenly Father will bring to fruition the desires he has placed within us.

Does this model of prayer line up with your life? Is your prayer life marked by abiding in him and his word first? Have you discovered the heartbeat of your heavenly Father? Do you feel as if you know how he feels about situations going on in your life? Are you so saturated with his word that it is transforming your actions, beliefs, emotions, and prayers?

Scripture says in Jeremiah 33:3, *"Call to me and I will answer you, and will tell you great and hidden things that you have not known."* 2 Corinthians 3:18 says, *"And we all, with unveiled face, beholding the glory of the Lord, are being transformed into the same image from one degree of glory to another. For this comes from the Lord who is the Spirit."* And Deuteronomy 4:29 says, *"But from there you will seek the Lord your God and you will find him, if you search after him with all your heart and with all your soul."* God longs for you to search out his heartbeat. He longs to reveal to you how he feels about you and every aspect of your life. He longs to transform your desires into his that you might desire and ask him for what is really best for you.

Asking God for something is meant to be as simple as abiding in his presence and word and praying in line with the desires he's birthed in you. Discover today the wealth of desires he longs to share with you. Ask him to show you how he feels and thinks. Saturate yourself in his word. Allow the teachings of Jesus to transform your perspectives. And ask your heavenly Father to bring to fruition the desires he's placed within you. May your desires be one with God's today as you spend time abiding in the true vine of Jesus.

GUIDED PRAYER

1. Meditate on Jesus' process of prayer. Reflect on each phrase. Allow the words of Jesus to transform the way you view spending time with God and prayer.

"If you abide in me, and my words abide in you, ask whatever you wish, and it will be done for you. By this my Father is glorified, that you bear much fruit and so prove to be my disciples." John 15:7-8

2. Spend time abiding in the presence and word of Jesus. Ask him to reveal how he feels about situations in your life where you need his help. Ask him to show you how he feels about anything you are curious about! Spending time with God is meant to consist of conversation, questions, and response. Seek and rest in his heart and word today.

"But from there you will seek the Lord your God and you will find him, if you search after him with all your heart and with all your soul." Deuteronomy 4:29

"Call to me and I will answer you, and will tell you great and hidden things that you have not known." Jeremiah 33:3

3. After discovering the heartbeat of God and the teachings of Jesus, ask God for your heart's desire in confidence! Petition your heavenly Father to bring to fruition the desires he is planting within you. Pray in line with the Spirit and Truth. Take joy in your heavenly Father's desire to answer your prayer.

"Continue steadfastly in prayer, being watchful in it with thanksgiving." Colossians 4:2

"And when you pray, you must not be like the hypocrites. For they love to stand and pray in the synagogues and at the street corners, that they may be seen by others. Truly, I say to you, they have received their reward. But when you pray, go into your room and shut the door and pray to your Father who is in secret. And your Father who sees in secret will reward you. And when you pray, do not heap up empty phrases as the Gentiles do, for they think that they will be heard for their many words. Do not be like them, for your Father knows what you need before you ask him." Matthew 6:5-8

The Lord loves to answer the prayers of his children. He longs to give you every good and perfect gift. Trust in his goodness. Have faith that he will respond to your prayers in more magnificent ways than you could ever imagine. He is our loving Father, and he loves to bless us. Rest in his presence and word today, and allow him to mold and shape you into the image of Jesus.

Extended Reading: Matthew 6

Abiding through Obedience

DAY 31

DEVOTIONAL

The concept of obedience has become shrouded with a connotation of negativity. When we think of obedience we normally infer a feeling of doing a task apart from a desire or longing. We associate obedience with obligation rather than fulfillment. But when Jesus walked on the earth he carried out a very different lifestyle of obedience. Jesus' life demonstrates what obedience to our heavenly Father is meant to look like. Obedience to God is choosing to live a lifestyle of love and devotion to our God who has loved us completely.

"As the Father has loved me, so have I loved you. Abide in my love. If you keep my commandments, you will abide in my love, just as I have kept my Father's commandments and abide in his love."

JOHN 15:9-10

Jesus says in John 15:9-10, *"As the Father has loved me, so have I loved you. Abide in my love. If you keep my commandments, you will abide in my love, just as I have kept my Father's commandments and abide in his love."* Too often we miss the heart of God when he calls us to obedience. Jesus illustrates here that he lived his life reciprocating the love he was shown by his Father. He lived his life in obedience to God out of the wealth of relationship he had, not out of obligation. And Jesus simply asks us to do the same. He invites us into the process of receiving and giving love as the foundation of our life that we might abide in the depth of relationship with our heavenly Father as he did.

In Luke 10:27, Jesus states the greatest commandments, *"You shall love the Lord your God with all your heart and with all your soul and with all your strength and with all your mind, and your neighbor as yourself."* How incredible is the heart of our God that he doesn't call us to a lifestyle of obligation or undesired sacrifice, but a lifestyle in which we reciprocate the vast love we've been shown in Christ to all the earth. God doesn't merely set rules before you but relationship as the goal. He's after your heart totally and completely.

In a world wrapped up in a self-seeking, self-satisfying agenda, God sets us free to step outside of the burden of ourselves and frees us to live for others. In a world wrought with the weight of pride, God pours out his unceasing, selfless love which has the power to transform us into children who abide in our heavenly Father. If we will choose to abide in God's commandments and love wholeheartedly, we will experience a satisfaction unknown to those with the attitude of selfishness and pride. We will experience the abundant life only those who abide in God can obtain.

So, abide in God's commandments today. Choose to live a lifestyle of wholehearted love of God and others. Choose to live in obedience to God in response to his amazing love. And discover the power, purpose, and freedom that comes from ministering to others with the very love you've been shown in Christ.

157

GUIDED PRAYER

1. Meditate on Jesus' process of prayer. Reflect on each phrase. Allow the words of Jesus to transform the way you view spending time with God and prayer.

"If you abide in me, and my words abide in you, ask whatever you wish, and it will be done for you. By this my Father is glorified, that you bear much fruit and so prove to be my disciples." John 15:7-8

2. Spend time abiding in the presence and word of Jesus. Ask him to reveal how he feels about situations in your life where you need his help. Ask him to show you how he feels about anything you are curious about! Spending time with God is meant to consist of conversation, questions, and response. Seek and rest in his heart and word today.

"But from there you will seek the Lord your God and you will find him, if you search after him with all your heart and with all your soul." Deuteronomy 4:29

"Call to me and I will answer you, and will tell you great and hidden things that you have not known." Jeremiah 33:3

3. After discovering the heartbeat of God and the teachings of Jesus, ask God for your heart's desire in confidence! Petition your heavenly Father to bring to fruition the desires he is planting within you. Pray in line with the Spirit and Truth. Take joy in your heavenly Father's desire to answer your prayer.

"Continue steadfastly in prayer, being watchful in it with thanksgiving." Colossians 4:2

"And when you pray, you must not be like the hypocrites. For they love to stand and pray in the synagogues and at the street corners, that they may be seen by others. Truly, I say to you, they have received their reward. But when you pray, go into your room and shut the door and pray to your Father who is in secret. And your Father who sees in secret will reward you. And when you pray, do not heap up empty phrases as the Gentiles do, for they think that they will be heard for their many words. Do not be like them, for your Father knows what you need before you ask him." Matthew 6:5-8

The Lord loves to answer the prayers of his children. He longs to give you every good and perfect gift. Trust in his goodness. Have faith that he will respond to your prayers in more magnificent ways than you could ever imagine. He is our loving Father, and he loves to bless us. Rest in his presence and word today, and allow him to mold and shape you into the image of Jesus.

Extended Reading: Matthew 6

Abiding in God's Friendship

DAY 32

DEVOTIONAL

Do you know that God calls you his friend? John 15:14-15 says, *"You are my friends if you do what I command you. No longer do I call you servants, for the servant does not know what his master is doing; but I have called you friends, for all that I have heard from my Father I have made known to you."* As a believer you have gained friendship with a God who exemplifies perfect, unconditional love. You have gained relationship with your Creator whose greatest desire is simply to spend time with you. Allow the love of your heavenly Father to sink in for a minute. Allow the Spirit to reveal to you God's motives today as we look at what it means for us to abide in the friendship of God.

"You are my friends if you do what I command you. No longer do I call you servants, for the servant does not know what his master is doing; but I have called you friends, for all that I have heard from my Father I have made known to you."

JOHN 15:14-15

John 15:13 says, *"Greater love has no one than this, that someone lay down his life for his friends."* Jesus committed the greatest act of love this world has ever known in laying down his life. And he did so willingly out of his desire for relationship with us. God desired friendship with you to the level that he would send his only Son to die in order to restore what sin had destroyed.

The questions before you today are: are you experiencing the fruits of friendship with Jesus? Are you receiving the satisfaction that comes from abiding in relationship with God? The Holy Spirit's desire today is to lead you into a greater depth of friendship with your Creator, the one who laid down his own life for your sake. What he asks of you today is to make time to invest in your friendship with him as you would any other relationship. He asks that you would value relationship with him to the level that you would commit time and energy to it. Just as marriage cannot be fruitful or enjoyable without investment from both parties, we must invest in our friendship with God to receive all that relationship with him is designed to bring us.

John 15:14 makes it clear that true friendship with God is following his commands. Jesus has revealed the pathway to abundant life. And he's led us to that path by laying down his own life that we might have the Holy Spirit working within us. To be friends with Jesus is to choose to lay down our own lives in response to his loving sacrifice. To walk in friendship with God is to choose humility over pride and follow the path set before us in Jesus. We are no longer servants unaware of the plans and will of our master, but friends who have heard, seen, and experienced the truth.

Will you choose friendship with God over the world today? Will you choose to follow the will of the God who laid down his life for yours? Will you walk down the pathway of life today, or will you choose to go your own way? True friendship with God is fully available to you today if you will follow the life-giving commandments of Jesus and make space and time to invest in your relationship with him. Nothing will bring you greater satisfaction than living out of the abundance of friendship with Jesus. Revelation 3:20 says, *"Behold, I stand at the door and knock. If anyone hears my voice and opens the door, I will come in to him and eat with him, and he with me."* Open the door of your heart to the God of love today and spend time fellowshipping with him.

161

GUIDED PRAYER

1. Meditate on your status as a friend of God. Allow Scripture to change your perspective on how God views you and how you should view God.

"You are my friends if you do what I command you. No longer do I call you servants, for the servant does not know what his master is doing; but I have called you friends, for all that I have heard from my Father I have made known to you." John 15:14-15

2. Reflect on your own life. What relationships do you invest in over your relationship with God? Who have you made the highest priority? In what ways are you not following the commands of Jesus?

"If anyone loves me, he will keep my word, and my Father will love him, and we will come to him and make our home with him." John 14:23

3. Repent of any way in which you have valued other relationships over God. Confess any ways in which you have not been following the commands of Jesus and receive the forgiveness of God. Spend time investing in your friendship now. Open the door of your heart and let God come in. Talk with him. Listen to him. Tell him how you feel. Spend time with him as you would another friend. Nothing could be more important than experiencing the abundance of friendship with God available to you in Christ.

"Behold, I stand at the door and knock. If anyone hears my voice and opens the door, I will come in to him and eat with him, and he with me." Revelation 3:20

"God is faithful, by whom you were called into the fellowship of his Son, Jesus Christ our Lord." 1 Corinthians 1:9

"I led them with cords of kindness, with the bands of love, and I became to them as one who eases the yoke on their jaws, and I bent down to them and fed them." Hosea 11:4

The only day we are promised is today. Don't wait to invest in your relationship with God. Don't set it aside while you take care of what seems to be more pressing. Loving God is always first priority. Spending time with him is always the most important thing. Choose to be a follower of Jesus who values his commands over any other. Choose his way over your own or the world's. Walk today with the fruit of friendship with God as your source and guide. If you do, you will experience favor and grace on even the most mundane tasks set before you. You will experience a foundation of love on which you have the grace to follow God wholeheartedly and love others purely and fully. Value friendship with God above all else and experience the abundant life available to you.

Extended Reading: 1 John 1-2

163

Abiding Fruit

DAY 33

DEVOTIONAL

You have been chosen and appointed to bear eternal and impactful fruit. John 15:16 says, *"You did not choose me, but I chose you and appointed you that you should go and bear fruit and that your fruit should abide."* God created all of us with a longing to make an important and lasting impact with the intention of satisfying that longing in him. He has a plan for your life that doesn't belong to anyone else. You alone can accomplish the works set before you, and you won't find true satisfaction until you do. Your heavenly Father has placed desires in you which he has plans to satisfy in magnificent and joyful ways. He knows for what purposes you were created and longs to lead you into a lifestyle of good works that will fill you with all the abundance of life available to you through Christ.

Ephesians 2:10 says, *"We are his workmanship, created in Christ Jesus for good works, which God prepared beforehand, that we should walk in them."* You were created to live a lifestyle of good works. It is not outside of your nature to accomplish amazing things no matter how you've lived your life up to this point. God takes what the world has deemed broken and useless and transforms it into the very likeness of his son, Jesus. He has plans to transform you into his disciple: ready, equipped, and useful for every good and fruitful work. Believe today that God would use you and discover the wealth of plans he has set before you. Surrender to the truth that God has better plans than you can ask or imagine in store for you if you will follow him. Come before him with expectation today, ready to receive all

"You did not choose me, but I chose you and appointed you that you should go and bear fruit and that your fruit should abide."

JOHN 15:16

the he would guide you to. Let's dive wholeheartedly into God's word and presence as we learn from him how to live the fruitful life he has appointed for us.

In order to bear the fruit God has set before us we must abide in him. Just as a branch cannot bear fruit without the nutrients the vine provides, we cannot bear fruit without being connected to our only source of true life, our heavenly Father. God leads us into the plans he has for us as we spend time in his presence and his word. Psalm 1:1-3 says,

Blessed is the man who walks not in the counsel of the wicked, nor stands in the way of sinners, nor sits in the seat of scoffers; but his delight is in the law of the Lord, and on his law he meditates day and night. He is like a tree planted by streams of water that yields its fruit in its season, and its leaf does not wither. In all that he does, he prospers.

It's in God's presence and word that we are molded, refined, and transformed. It's only in spending time with him that we become nourished and ready to bear fruit. Just as a tree must be pruned in order to bear more fruit, we must allow God to tear away parts of our life that are keeping us from the good works he intends for us. We must spend time in God's presence being fashioned, healed, and transformed.

In order to bear the fruit God intends, we must learn to allow the Spirit to work in and through us. God not only transforms us as we spend time with him and his word, but empowers us through the Holy Spirit to do good works we could never accomplish in our own strength. It's only through God working in us that our weaknesses are turned into strengths so we can truly love one another. And it's only through the Spirit that hearts are changed and drawn to our heavenly Father. God longs to give you his heart for people. He longs to empower you to speak and work with his authority. He longs to do works through you that can't be explained except by his reality. If you will choose to humble yourself before God and allow him to work in and through you, you will begin to bear the very fruit of the Holy Spirit dwelling within you. The disciples had no great gifts or power on their own. It was only by the working of the Holy Spirit that Christianity exploded in size and influence and changed the world. Co-labor with the Holy Spirit in all that you do. Allow him to move and work in every part of your life and experience all the incredible ways he desires to use you to bring the kingdom of God to earth.

Spend time abiding in the true vine of God today. Open your heart and mind to his word. And allow the Holy Spirit to teach you how he desires to work in and through you. May the amazing plans God has for you bring peace, purpose, and joy to your life today.

GUIDED PRAYER

1. Meditate on God's desire to produce important and lasting fruit through your life.

"You did not choose me, but I chose you and appointed you that you should go and bear fruit and that your fruit should abide." John 15:16

"For we are his workmanship, created in Christ Jesus for good works, which God prepared beforehand, that we should walk in them." Ephesians 2:10

2. Spend time in God's presence allowing him to nourish and empower you for good works. Ask him to reveal what he has set before you to accomplish for his kingdom today. Ask the Holy Spirit to work in and through you.

"Blessed is the man who walks not in the counsel of the wicked, nor stands in the way of sinners, nor sits in the seat of scoffers; but his delight is in the law of the Lord, and on his law he meditates day and night. He is like a tree planted by streams of water that yields its fruit in its season, and its leaf does not wither. In all that he does, he prospers." Psalm 1:1-3

"And let us not grow weary of doing good, for in due season we will reap, if we do not give up." Galatians 6:9

3. Commit to following the leadership of the Holy Spirit today as he guides you to producing good fruit. Choose to love others as God has loved you. Choose to live a lifestyle of agreeing with the Holy Spirit in every way that he leads you.

How vast is God's love for us that he would not only save us, redeem us, and set us free, but he desires to use us, a broken and needy people, to change the world. God desires to anoint his people with his Spirit to accomplish his work. May your life be marked by the wonderful and lasting fruit of a child of God surrendered to and in love with our heavenly Father.

Extended Reading: Romans 8

God Prunes Us in His Love

DAY 34

DEVOTIONAL

The world teaches that discipline is about shaming us into acting perfectly. Discipline from the world usually comes from a place of selfishness rather than love, a pursuit of perfection rather than godliness, and intends to lead us to the appearance of morality rather than molding and shaping the heart. For this reason, we so often run away from the discipline of our heavenly Father. But, Hebrews 12:5-6 says, *"My son, do not regard lightly the discipline of the Lord, nor be weary when reproved by him. For the Lord disciplines the one he loves, and chastises every son whom he receives."* God loves us, so he disciplines us. He has such incredible plans for us that he must mold and shape us into children ready and equipped for authority, influence, and the power of the Spirit. His discipline is always intended to lead us to abundant life, not to tear us down or shame us. As we look at God's desire to discipline us, allow his love to open your heart and lead you into the process of pruning intended solely to refine, help, and produce fruit in you.

John 15:2 says, *"Every branch in me that does not bear fruit he takes away, and every branch that does bear fruit he prunes, that it may bear more fruit."* The only way for us to bear more fruit in God is to allow him to prune us. The pursuit and cares of the world are like weeds that crowd out and steal nourishment from the good, fruitful branches rooted in God. God's plan is to prune, heal and transform us into children who live in the world but are not of it (John 17:14-19). He longs to tear down the strongholds of pride and sin that have kept us from experiencing the fullness of his promises. And he plans to lead us to a lifestyle of important and eternal fruit which will fill us with the fullness of joy.

So how do we allow God to prune us? How can we engage in his process of healing and transformation? It all starts with seeing the depth of his love for us. Psalm 103:2-4 says, *"Bless the Lord, O my soul, and forget not all his benefits, who forgives all your iniquity, who heals all your diseases, who redeems your life from the pit, who crowns you with steadfast love and mercy."* God's process of discipline is so different than the world's because it is all rooted in his unconditional love for us. In order to consistently engage in his loving discipline, we must consistently encounter his love. We have to spend time with the all-loving heart of our heavenly Father to separate his discipline

"Every branch in me that does not bear fruit he takes away, and every branch that does bear fruit he prunes, that it may bear more fruit."

from the unloving discipline of so many of our earthly fathers. His discipline is always solely for our benefit and completely to our good. In order for us to fully give ourselves over to his discipline, we must have continual revelation of the depth of his love for us.

Next we have to choose his ways over the ways of the world. We have to sacrifice what we thought mattered for what he says matters. Romans 12:1 says, *"I appeal to you therefore, brothers, by the mercies of God, to present your bodies as a living sacrifice, holy and acceptable to God, which is your spiritual worship."* His discipline will be painful because it will lead you to look different from the world you grew up in. He will take our living sacrifice of the world's opinions and transform us into children who solely value his opinion. Most of us have valued the ways and opinions of the world so highly that living apart from them feels completely foreign and frightening. So we must choose to trust God over what we have understood to be important or valuable. God will lead all of us to a lifestyle of humility in opposition to the world's values of pride and success. He will lead all of us to a lifestyle of loving others rather than getting all we can out of

others. He will lead all of us to a lifestyle of dependence on him rather than self-empowerment. And he will most certainly lead all of us to a life of relationship with him as our highest priority over the opinions and friendship of others. Every piece of the pruning process is difficult. But, every time you agree with and follow the Holy Spirit through the process you will come out more satisfied, joyful, free, empowered, and fruitful than you were before. Hebrews 12:11 says, *"For the moment all discipline seems painful rather than pleasant, but later it yields the peaceful fruit of righteousness to those who have been trained by it."* After you throw off the weight of the world you will wonder how you ever lived under its burden.

Engage with your loving heavenly Father in the process of pruning. Open your heart and allow him to tear down the walls that have been keeping you from experiencing the flood of abundant life and works he has planned for you. See his love and respond to it by sacrificing your ways of thinking and living. He has plans to heal, transform, and free you today if you will simply follow the leadership of the Holy Spirit through the pruning process.

GUIDED PRAYER

1. Meditate on God's desire to prune you. Reflect on how God's discipline is always rooted in his love. Compare God's desire to discipline you to the world's desire. Separate his desire from other discipline you have received in the past if it wasn't done with his heart.

"My son, do not regard lightly the discipline of the Lord, nor be weary when reproved by him. For the Lord disciplines the one he loves, and chastises every son whom he receives." Hebrews 12:5-6

"For the moment all discipline seems painful rather than pleasant, but later it yields the peaceful fruit of righteousness to those who have been trained by it." Hebrews 12:11

"Whoever spares the rod hates his son, but he who loves him is diligent to discipline him." Proverbs 13:34

2. Open your heart to the Spirit and ask him to tear away any parts of your life that are not bearing the fruit of God. Follow his leadership as you think about parts of your lifestyle that aren't filled with the abundant life God desires. What does he want to change about your perspective, time, or relationships? What is he asking you to do or give up so that you might live more freely, empowered, and fruitfully? Take as much time to listen to the Spirit as you need.

"He saved us, not because of works done by us in righteousness, but according to his own mercy, by the washing of regeneration and renewal of the Holy Spirit." Titus 3:5

"Bless the Lord, O my soul, and forget not all his benefits, who forgives all your iniquity, who heals all your diseases, who redeems your life from the pit, who crowns you with steadfast love and mercy." Psalm 103:2-4

3. Agree with his pruning and follow through with whatever he is leading you to do. Make plans to cut out of your life anything he has revealed to you. Call a friend and ask for accountability to hold you to the discipline God has for you. Commit to engaging in the process of discipline on an ongoing basis so that God can continually transform any areas of your life that are hurting you rather than guiding you to abundant life in your heavenly Father.

"I appeal to you therefore, brothers, by the mercies of God, to present your bodies as a living sacrifice, holy and acceptable to God, which is your spiritual worship." Romans 12:1

One of the greatest gifts of the Holy Spirit we can receive is a desire to be disciplined and pruned by our heavenly Father. May we all have the heart of the Psalmist who wrote in Psalm 51:10-12,

Create in me a clean heart, O God, and renew a right spirit within me. Cast me not away from your presence, and take not your Holy Spirit from me. Restore to me the joy of your salvation, and uphold me with a willing spirit.

Extended Reading: Hebrews 12

170

Abiding in God's Joy

DAY 35

DEVOTIONAL

The kingdom of our God is one of joy, rejoicing, and gladness (Romans 14:17). Our heavenly Father is the one who throws a massive party for the prodigal returned home (Luke 15:11-32). He's the God of the angels who rejoices over one sinner who repents (Luke 15:10). He's the God who celebrates with us, sings over us, and rejoices in us (Zephaniah 3:17). And at the end of this age he will throw a wedding feast in celebration of the joy he has over total restored relationship with us, his bride (Revelation 19:6-9).

Scripture is clear that our God doesn't desire to keep his joy to himself, but longs to fill us with it to overflowing. Toward the end of the John 15:1-17 passage we have been studying this week, Jesus says, *"These things I have spoken to you, that my joy may be in you, and that your joy may be full"* (John 15:11). God's plan is to fill us with the fullness of joy that is grounded solely in him rather than the ever-changing circumstances around us. That's why Galatians 5:22 tells us that, *"The fruit of the Spirit is . . . joy."* Joy is meant to come from the Holy Spirit within us. It's in relationship with God that we experience his abundant joy. Let's go wholeheartedly into the heart of God today and find the reservoir of joy he longs to guide us to. Let's be believers marked by the joy of our heavenly Father rather than the dissatisfaction we experience from the world.

So how do we experience the joy of God? How can the joy of Jesus be in us as he spoke of in John 15:11? Philippians 4:4: *"Rejoice in the Lord always; again I will*

*"These things I have spoken to you, that my joy
may be in you, and that your joy may be full."*

JOHN 15:11

say, Rejoice." As children of God we must rejoice in our heavenly Father above all else. There is always joy to be found when our highest priority is God. Our God is always turning what the enemy meant for evil into our good if we will choose to love him above all else (Romans 8:28). When we lean on God as the source of our contentment rather than the opinion of man or success in the world, we will have a sure foundation on which to experience joy. But, when our emotions change with the tides of the world, our joy will come and go like the waves. Ground yourself in God. Rejoice in the Lord always because he's always worthy of rejoicing in. And in placing him first you will experience vast and unshakable joy.

To experience the fullness of joy God has for us we must also trust in his plans. Psalm 118:24 says, *"This is the day that the Lord has made; let us rejoice and be glad in it."* Each day of our life was created by God. And while the world operates apart from his leadership, when we trust in him and allow him to work in and through us he takes circumstances that would normally harm us and turns them into miraculous examples of his unceasing love. Acts 16:25-26 tells us a story in which Paul and Silas exemplify a lifestyle of trusting in God. Scripture says, *"About midnight Paul and Silas were praying and singing hymns to God, and*

the prisoners were listening to them, and suddenly there was a great earthquake, so that the foundations of the prison were shaken. And immediately all the doors were opened, and everyone's bonds were unfastened." Paul and Silas knew that God can and will work in our lives when we place our trust in him. So they were able to praise and worship God in joy through any circumstance, and God did the miraculous. James describes this principle in James 1:2-4 when he writes, *"Count it all joy, my brothers, when you meet trials of various kinds, for you know that the testing of your faith produces steadfastness. And let steadfastness have its full effect, that you may be perfect and complete, lacking in nothing."* We can have joy in trial when we trust in God and live for him above all else.

You and I were not created solely for this world. Our home is with our heavenly Father in heaven. Unceasing joy comes from living with the perspective of God rather than the world. Rejoicing comes from trusting that our God is perfectly loving, perfectly real, and perfectly powerful. Spend time in God's presence experiencing his joy. Allow the Spirit to bear the fruit of joy in your life. Trust in God alone to bring about all that he has planned for you and live your life on the unshakable foundation of his love and joy today.

GUIDED PRAYER

1. Meditate on God's desire to fill you with abounding joy.

"These things I have spoken to you, that my joy may be in you, and that your joy may be full." John 15:11

"For the kingdom of God is not a matter of eating and drinking but of righteousness and peace and joy in the Holy Spirit." Romans 14:17

"But the fruit of the Spirit is love, joy, peace, patience, kindness, goodness, faithfulness." Galatians 5:22

2. Reflect on your own life. Where are you not experiencing joy? What do you think is stealing your joy in those areas? Ask the Spirit to lead you into the fullness of joy in every area of your life. Trust him as he guides you into a life of faith and submission to God.

"Until now you have asked nothing in my name. Ask, and you will receive, that your joy may be full." John 16:24

3. Receive the joy of Jesus. Rejoice in him. Rejoice in his plans for your day. Thank him for his love and desire to celebrate in you. Spend time resting in his joyful and peaceful presence.

"Rejoice in the Lord always; again I will say, Rejoice." Philippians 4:4

"This is the day that the Lord has made; let us rejoice and be glad in it." Psalm 118:24

"A joyful heart is good medicine, but a crushed spirit dries up the bones." Proverbs 17:22

Seek out the joy of your heavenly Father all day today. When you begin to feel down, burdened, or depressed, spend time rejoicing in God. Allow God to reveal to you his heart for situations in your life. Respond to hard times with celebration in the fact that God will turn what was meant for evil into good if you will commit yourself to his plans and purposes. God's plan is to fill you with unceasing joy every day of your life. He longs to lay a foundation of his love for you every morning so that you can go out into your day filled with unshakable joy. May his promise in Isaiah 55:12 come to fruition in your life today:

For you shall go out in joy and be led forth in peace; the mountains and the hills before you shall break forth into singing, and all the trees of the field shall clap their hands.

Extended Reading: Isaiah 55